*"This book is dedicated my mother, the late Shirley Collins, and all the single parents of the world.*

*May your children one day appreciate your struggles and the good Lord smile upon you."*

**~ Larry McCoy ~**

# FATHERLESS

A Novel

by Larry McCoy

Printed in the United States of America

Fatherless is a work of fiction. Names, main characters and
places are fictitiously used. Any resemblance of events
and incidents are coincidental.

Copyright © 2020

Paperback ISBN: 978-0-9702069-3-0
Ebook ISBN: 978-0-9702069-4-7
www.lombooks.me
First Edition

Cover Designer: Tracarris Wince
Editing: YCH, Inc

Turner Lawrence Cook Publishing
P O Box 11596
Jackson, MS 39283

www.lombooks.me
601.214.1497
Larrymccoy1@aol.com

# FATHERLESS

# TABLE OF CONTENTS

*"There was a boy*
*A very strange enchanted boy...*
*...The greatest thing you'll ever learn*
*Is just to love and be loved in return."*

— *Nat King Cole*

FATHERLESS

# 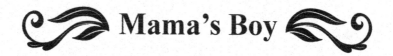 Mama's Boy

The year of 1958 had not been Wilma Ann Carter's best. She was short, fat, and cross-eyed with very soft reddish curly hair that resembled a dense mat sitting on top of her head. Her crazy, violent ex-husband had just left her again, this time moving only a couple of miles up the road from the small, whitewashed shotgun home he shared with Wilma Ann and their nine-year-old daughter Retha. This final breakup occurred after Wilma Ann had endured 10 years of his abusive behavior and decided enough was enough. She finally put a bullet hole in him, hitting his shoulder, a few inches away from his heart. As Wilma Ann gathered up Retha and their meager belongings to head to her parents' home, her ex-husband hurled vicious threats at her and swore that one day he would get her back for shooting him. Wilma Ann believed him.

Mysteriously and shortly after the move, the home of Wilma Ann's parents burned to the ground. Arson was clearly the cause, yet, no one was ever arrested for the crime. Although the family survived without harm to their physical bodies, the fire destroyed all the belongings of Wilma Ann, her children and her parents, including $5,000 in cash kept in the master bedroom's huge fluffy feathered mattress.

While her ex-husband's threats gave her much reason for continued concern, life moved on for Wilma Ann. She stopped looking over her shoulder when she met Otis. She believed with all her heart the he was the true love of her life. A tall, strong, quiet and somber man, Otis was a transplant to the Mississippi Delta from a community just outside of Memphis in Shelby County, Tennessee. Although an only child, both his father and mother lost their respective jobs as machinist and seamstress during America's historic financial crisis that started in 1929 and lingered into the 1930s.

Otis was only five years old when his unemployed father deserted the family to search for a job in St. Louis, Missouri. He never saw his father again. However, Otis went on to finish the eighth grade at the Shaw Colored Training School before his mother met her second husband. He convinced her to bring her son and join him for a new life in the Mississippi Delta. Constantly in dispute with his stepfather, Otis ran away from home at the age of 14. He hated sharecropping and built a portfolio of on-the-job skills that ranged from prize fighting to mechanic to ranching. Otis and Wilma Ann met during one of their visits to Sweet's Place, a Mississippi Delta juke joint. They danced, talked, ate Sweet's fried porkchop sandwiches, drank colas and found in that one night that they were meant for each other. Within weeks, the two moved in together and made their home on Hobbs Plantation.

As common law marriage partners, Wilma Ann and Otis continued living in the rural Mississippi Delta and expanded their family with an addition of two sons, Arthur and Otha, and another daughter, Mae. Abruptly, something went wrong in their seemingly settled family life. Wilma Ann's support and husband Otis suddenly left Wilma Ann and their children high and dry.

With the man of their family gone, Wilma Ann was forced to figure out how to raise her four children as the sole bread winner on a sharecropping income. Young Arthur sat on a tree stump wishing for Otis and reflecting on how his family often ended up drawing life's short straws. His mind settled on the warm thought of his daddy returning to rescue his family from such a hard life.

FATHERLESS

As with most blacks living in the Mississippi Delta, Wilma Ann's family endured some hard and terrifying times. It wasn't that long ago that an all-white jury in Tallahatchie County acquitted two white men of the lynching and brutal murder of the 14-year-old black boy named Emmett Till. The freed murderers alleged that their victim whistled at a white woman in a little hamlet called Money, Mississippi. The fallout from the heinous crime exposed and highlighted the fragile social structure of black and white citizens. The crime also brought attention to the peonage relationship that generally existed between wealthy white plantation owners and poor black sharecroppers. The Jim Crow South seemed content in having shown the world that "they could kill a nigga and get away with it." With much distrust of whites, black families ramped up teaching their sons to avoid contact with whites as much as possible, especially white females. At the same time, most whites continued to assert their white supremacy beliefs.

The phrase "remember Emmett Till" was an ominous warning to all black males. Wilma Ann had been warning her eldest son Arthur of this danger for three years, since he was five years old--the age Arthur was when Emmett Till's was pulled from the muddy waters of the Tallahatchie River. Maybe her overprotectiveness and nagging of Arthur was because he was her first son. It was a fact that the atrocious beating, mutilation and abuse shown widely to the world in Jet, Ebony and Life magazines were forever etched in her mind. The next time some evil white men wanted to show their power, her son's dead body--lynched and hung from a tree or thrown into a murky river--could be the result. For Arthur, his mother's close watch on him earned him the reputation of being a "mama's boy."

When he was two years old, Arthur experienced a traumatic health issue while sitting between his parents Wilma Ann and Otis in the front seat of their 1949 maple brown Nash automobile. Little Arthur loved to sit on the thick soft cloth seat and listen to Wilma Ann and Otis talk as they rode. Suddenly, Arthur's hernia ruptured and tore a hole in his stomach. Wilma Ann had to push Arthur's intestines back in his stomach as Otis sped to the hospital in the nearby Town of Mound Bayou. At the all-black town's Taborian Hospital, Dr. Searcy Walker performed an emergency surgery to repair Arthur's hernia and torn belly. Afterward, he wrapped thick bandages around Arthur's stomach to support holding his intestines in place. Dr. Walker advised Wilma Ann and Otis to restrict their son's activities for at least six months to prevent another hernia tear. During his recovery, Arthur's stomach hurt constantly and he lost his appetite. Consequently, Arthur became an anemic, skinny child. His frailty earned Arthur a new name that stuck with him throughout his childhood. Arthur's family and friends now called him by the nickname his uncle gave him--"Bird."

Wilma Ann did not allow Bird any unsupervised contacts with other children. She always tried to keep him with her. Despite Bird's ability to walk and run without any problems, his mother explained that she would carry him in her arms as much as possible. However, she had to stop picking him up and carrying him around like a baby when her son had grown so tall that his feet started dragging on the ground. These demonstrations made the mama's boy reference was hard to shake. Even when Bird got into trouble, Wilma Ann would not let his daddy Otis punish him with a whipping as was typical punishment for most black children in the 1950s. Many times, Bird took advantage of those situations. For example, one day, Bird ate an entire watermelon that his daddy had brought home to be served as dessert for one of their meals. Otis wanted to spank Bird for his gluttony and lack of consideration for his parents and siblings. Wilma

Ann hid Bird from his father and a silent, triumphant smile spread across the "mama's boy" face. Not only did people around Bird recognize him as a mama's boy, apparently Bird himself knew it, too, and took solace in being the quintessential mama's boy.

FATHERLESS

 **Night Crawlers**

Bird had a difficult time sleeping at night. A light sleeper, often the slightest noise or movement would awaken him. As in most cramped sharecropping households across the South, children usually slept two or three to a bed. Boys slept together in one bed while girls slept together in another bed. Small children and babies slept with their parents. Both long-legged and lanky, Arthur and his younger brother Otha slept in the same bed. Their bed was a sofa during the day and at bedtime, its back was lowered to the same height as the seat to become a full-size bed. Frustrating his brother's effort to rest, Otha tended to sleep on his knees and rearrange their cover by pulling the sheets under him. When the room's coal oil lamp lights were turned off, the noisy rats took over, continuously scurrying across the floor and making gnawing sounds as the nocturnal rodents chewed on walls and stuff inside the aging structure. From time to time, a rat would leap from a window sill onto Bird's bed.

He and his siblings worried the vermin might bite them. This fear kept Bird scratching throughout the night.

Sure, the rats were troublesome enough, but the mosquitoes and irritating flies were just as bad. The bloodsucking mosquitoes kept Bird awake, too. When he swatted them, the ones that didn't get away were so full of blood extracted from both humans and animals that they released bubbles of blood that stained Bird's clothes, bed coverings or on whatever material where they were found and squashed to death. Better dead mosquitoes than a dead child, thought Bird. At least, the bothersome flies did not usually bite Bird or keep him awake like the rats and mosquitoes. However, the flies were a nuisance and regularly gathered around outhouses and dead animals. Somehow finding ways to get past the screened doors, the flies irritated Bird, too. Not only did they pose a health hazard, but they tried to get into Bird's mouth and nose. He often slept with his bedspread over his head, despite it reeking of the Black Flag insect killer spray that Otis released into the air and about their home several times during the night. Sold as a deadly insect spray, the swarms of mosquitoes in the cotton fields that surrounded and entered their home were undeterred by the mists of Black Flag. However, there were some rare times, just before and immediately after daybreak, when the rats, flies, mosquitoes and other pests quieted down and allowed Bird to get some of his best sleep.

FATHERLESS

 **Wilma Ann**

One Monday morning, Bird was half awake, and vaguely remembered saying something to his mama about his dad. He heard Wilma Ann respond, "Boy, I done tole ya he ain't heah, he been gone, he gon ta see a main bout a damn job. Now, take yo liddle narrow ass back ta sleep and quit axing me da same thangs over and over. Hell, ya know he ain't in my skin. He'll be back when he gits back." Bird had never heard his mama curse or even criticize him. That day, Bird learned what most people already knew about Wilma Ann—that she could string a group of insulting words together that would curl a horse's hair and she would fill the insults with the necessary "cuss" words to drive home her point.

Bird tried to go back to sleep, but he felt uneasy. His mama's face revealed a sense of sadness and distress that triggered a numbness in his head. Wilma

Ann grabbed an old shirt and made a snorting sound as she blew her nose into it and used another part of the shirt to wipe tears from her left eye. She must have felt the sensation of tears swelling in her right eye, but those tear ducts had been blocked since her childhood years. As a single tear rolled down his mother's left cheek, Bird knew his family was about to face some very deep problems. His grandparents told him that when she was a small child, Wilma Ann usually played alone, talked to herself and insisted that she and God were friends. As his mama started moaning her version of "The Old Rugged Cross," Bird started his own quiet prayer that Wilma Ann would snap out her scary mental state because he and his siblings needed an adult Wilma Ann, not a six-year-old for a mama! Bird knew Wilma Ann was back in her childhood as she mumbled an offbeat, "Jesus, keep me near the cross, precious Lawd, take my hane, lead me on, let me stand." She transitioned to a long loud wail in the middle of her singing and moaning. While his mama was howling to the top of her lungs, Bird wondered why so many church people thought his mother had great musical vocal abilities.

Bird closed his eyes and pulled his bedspread tightly over his head. He detested her singing! His mother barely remembered the lyrics to any songs, and she developed a knack for creatively inserting her own words. This habit of hers consistently produced another version of the same song. She was apparently tone deaf with a raspy, twangy and unappealing voice. Plus, her timing was a half-beat late. Only the uninformed attempted to try to sing with her. Yet, most of the churches in the Asher, Mississippi, area regularly invited her to sing at funerals and revivals. Wilma Ann's uncanny gift for comforting "the bereaved" and entertaining those present. In Bird's opinion, his mama's current rendition was not bringing any comfort or peace to him or his siblings.

In fact, just like she enjoyed her reputation as a vocalist, Wilma Ann also took pride in her reputation as a "prayer warrior," too, despite on occasion, going to church to whip another woman's butt. She was also very adept at using her teeth to remove bottle caps from soda bottles and ringing the heads off live chickens. Wilma Ann had a reputation on the Hobbs plantation as the most audacious black woman on the farm. She was intelligent and had a gift for gab. The white folks said Wilma Ann could sell snow to an Eskimo. She claimed that she picked 400 pounds of cotton on Saturday, "hatched" Arthur (Bird) on Sunday, and picked extra cotton the next day.

FATHERLESS

Wilma Ann was born in Sharkey County, Mississippi, to a nurturing family who earned a Mississippi Delta black man's above-average income due to her father being the foreman of a large plantation. Yet, Wilma Ann boasted that she was born in Hard Times, Mississippi, and "ate rocks and drank sand for breakfast." Most folks who met or heard of her thought she was a little mentally "off her rocker." Wilma Ann helped to perpetuate the myth by claiming a mule kicked her in the head when she was three years old. Since she didn't die from the kick, it obviously had made her better with a power to see visions and interpret signs. "Afta all, the Lawd says what don't kill ya, make ya stronger," she boasted.

The day Bird woke up asking the whereabouts of his father, Wilma Ann prayed, "Jesus, I feel lack I'm inna knife fight wit a short stick. I knoe I got a long row ta hoe, but I truss ya ta make it alright, Dis is jest a tes lack ya tessed Abraham, tes yo servant Lloyd, ya sey yo yoke is easy but plez make it easier on me an my chilluns. Plenti folks round dis plantation need chestizing. Plez let sum lightin strik summa dem ta show ya ain't fooling round. keep da North star out ta night fur me in case yo servant needs ta leave dis place inna hurry. Amen."

FATHERLESS

Bird barely recognized the woman he knew as his mother. Uncharacteristically, Wilma Ann looked small and frail as she slowly swiped a cluster of dried tear stains from beneath her left eye. She took some washing powder and carefully used both her hands to lift the slop jar that was sitting near her bed and shuffled out the back door to empty the waste. She poured out the urine and other previous night excrement from the slop jar on to the ground behind the family's outhouse. Instead of her ritual of disposing the waste in the outhouse toilet, rinsing the container at the pump and bringing it back into the house, she just dumped the slop jar and its contents there on the ground. On her way back into the house, Wilma Ann bent over the rusty outdoor hand water pump, primed it with a few handle pushes and felt the cool water flow on her hands. She mixed in a portion of detergent powder, washed her hands, and went back into her house. She walked out of the kitchen into the front room. Barely putting one foot in front of the other, his mother's shoulders slouched so far that they appeared to fold inward and crush her bosom.

FATHERLESS

# 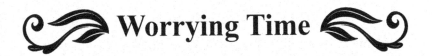 Worrying Time

Harvest time was at its peak for the cotton-picking season and Wilma Ann was readying herself to go to her sun-up-to-sun-down-job the cotton field. Wilma Ann was a legendary cotton picker. The average person had a good day if he or she picked about 175 pounds of cotton. Convicts from the Mississippi State Prison were forced to pick 250 pounds of cotton per day. Wilma Ann picked more than 400 pounds of cotton per day. At $2.50 pay per 100 pounds of cotton picked, she earned $10 a day for picking cotton and a little over three dollars per day for chopping cotton. Of course, as sharecroppers, housing was included, albeit it substandard. Utilities provided certainly did not include electricity. Water came from a hand pump and sewer service was a a sharecropper-built outhouse—sort of a wooden seat placed over a hole in the ground. Also provided to sharecroppers at each shotgun house was a woodburning stove for cooking, heating bath water and warming the structure during the cold season. Charges on a food account at the plantation store would be deducted from each sharecropper family's total earnings.

As most experienced cotton choppers and pickers did every workday, Wilma Ann donned several layers of clothing. The layers helped field laborers toiling in high temperatures and bright sun rays protect their skin, trap perspiration in their garb and keep them cool. Wilma Ann's red checkered head rag was tied tightly around her mat of red hair and she wore men's blue jeans under a green skirt. Thick white socks, brown discolored tennis shoes and two dingy white oversized tee shirts completed her outfit for picking cotton. As Bird watched her dress and pace about, he knew something was not quite right.

In contrast to her weekday work attire, Sundays earned Wilma Ann the title of being the best adorned black woman living on the Hobbs plantation. Although not her time to style and profile, his mama always held her head up high. Yet, this morning, Arthur saw her with her head still bowed as she pulled out the top two drawers of her dresser. Rats scurried out as Wilma Ann clutched and sniffed two of Otis' old plaid shirts. She briefly examined them for damage. "Damn rats, dey gittin fat on dis rat poison. Dey eatin it lack its candy," she said. Wilma

Ann pulled the two plaid shirts on over the two t-shirts she already was wearing. She used another shirt that had holes in it to wipe the mucus from her nose as she seemed to be about to cry. She rubbed her cheek, where tears ordinarily would have fallen had she not been a longtime sufferer of the dry eye disorder and the strabismus that made her eyes focus in opposite directions. Wilma Ann was sweating but she kept raising her hands up and down and pacing about the kitchen. Bird and his siblings' concern turned to full-blown worry the moment their mother went back to humming and singing varied stanzas of several gospel renditions.

# 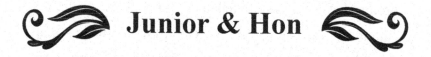 Junior & Hon

John L. Hobbs, Jr., whom everyone called Junior, owned the plantation where Arthur and his family lived. Hon and other drivers on the Hobbs's farm were responsible for hauling tenant workers and sharecroppers to and from the cotton fields. Hon's proper name was Hondo Howell. He was very short-tempered and impatient. Hon expected anyone wanting to ride to work in the fields to be waiting at the edge of their dirt packed yards as he arrived in front of their home.

People seem to think Hon's stank attitude was about his perceived demotion on Hobbs plantation. Hon had spent many years as Junior's driver and confidant. Junior also used Hon as his eyes and ears in the black community. Although Hon was only 62 years old, he had lived on the Hobbs plantation for nearly 50 of those years. He used a mixture of lye and jet-black dye in his hair to make it dark and wavy. No longer a chauffeur for Junior, Hon still dressed in crisply starched and ironed tan khaki pants and a matching long-sleeved shirt. His brown Stacy Adams shoes were always clean and sported a mirror-like shine. Hon and Junior often "drank" liquor together and Hon believed that Junior truly loved him. Junior had once put his arm around Hon's shoulders and said, "Hon, I lack dranking with you mo den I do my own color."

Unfortunately, the two drinking buddies found discord in their relationship when Hon fell asleep while he was driving Junior on a trip to Forest, Mississippi. While taking a curve too fast, the beautiful and impressive Fleetwood Cadillac hit a truck carrying live chickens and flipped over two times. Except for some chickens and dozens of eggs, none of the drivers and passengers involved in the crash suffered any significant injuries. Sadly, however, this wreck was Hon's fifth automobile accident during the last four years. Each accident showed both Hon and Junior were drunk. Junior placed the entire blame on Hon and, consequently, decided that it was in their mutual best interest for Hon to retire from chauffeur work.

Because of his deep affection for Hon, Junior allowed Hon to borrow his used pickup truck so he could continue to earn a living. Hon's new job duties were transporting plantation workers to and from the cotton fields and supervising their work. In his role as one of the plantation's "straw bosses," Hon earned five dollars per day, a dollar more than he earned as Junior's chauffeur. Yet, Hon felt demeaned and demoted in his new position as he packed up to 16 people on side benches in the truck bed and four more on its floor.

Wilma Ann and Otis had worked and lived on the Hobbs plantation for almost three years. With more than 7,000 acres of prime rural Mississippi Delta farmland, the Hobbs property was one of the smaller farms in the region. Tenants living on the Hobbs plantation had to arrive for work at the designated jobsite by six o'clock every weekday and Saturday morning. The plantation social order among black workers generally consisted of high-ranking house maids, chauffeurs/handymen, shop workers, tractor drivers, straw bosses and finally, the low-ranking field hands.

Arthur's father Otis was a tractor driver/ shop worker and his mother Wilma Ann was a field hand. Most of the people of color who worked on the Hobbs place were uneducated and illiterate. In fact, public schooling was quite limited and inadequate for most people living and working as sharecroppers in the Mississippi Delta during the 1950s (even after

FATHERLESS

the historic Brown vs. Board of Education decision by the Supreme Court requiring school desegregation and funding equity.) The sharecroppers lived in old, dilapidated shotgun houses located on parcels of land near the fields they worked. Most of the housing quarters had no plumbing or electricity. Outhouses served as permanent toilets, pumps had to be primed to produce water for cooking and cleaning, and wood fires in iron stoves sat in kitchen areas to not only use for cooking, but also for heating bath water and warming the entire typical three-room house. The public school for the children of sharecroppers on the Hobbs plantation was not much better. Southern black schools received barely half of the per-pupil funding as the white schools. As the one in Bird's community, most of the black schools lacked cafeterias, libraries, gymnasiums, running water and electricity. Otis was considered very fortunate to have gone to school in the Memphis area and to have completed the eighth grade.

The Hobbs plantation was more than a century old and had thrived during slavery and with the help of tenant labor and a peonage system, it was still thriving in the 1950s. Junior lived in a huge white antebellum mansion that was graced by acres of landscapes of the prettiest flowers, manicured grass and hedges, and beautiful magnolias, oaks, elms and a variety of other trees. The sharecropper shotgun homes were located away from the stately mansion off dirt or rocky roads and on soiled packed so tight grass wouldn't grow there. Their yards had no grass. Made of packed hard dirt, the yards were usually swept clean with a broom. The tenant workers' homes were faded, unpainted or whitewashed wood frame structures topped with tin roofs. The inside spaces formed an opened sight line that would allow a person with a shotgun to shoot straight through. (Thus, came the name of shotgun houses.) The plantation owners reportedly like the design because they could be at the front of the house and see everything all the way to the last room. There were no hallways or closed doors except for the front door to enter the house and the back door that lead to the outhouse toilet.

The floors of the shotgun houses were aged mix-matched two by four boards nailed to a wooden frame beneath the house. Most had at least one window on each side of the structures. Families used the front and middle rooms as bedrooms and the back rooms as a kitchen. Their water pump was in the front yard and the outhouse with a wooden commode over a hole in the ground was located behind the shotgun house.

FATHERLESS

Hobbs grouped most of the "colored" families on his plantation in settlements--groups of shotgun houses close together. Tight-knit communities were formed by the residents out of necessity. Each settlement house was about 15 yards away from the next home. Many relatives lived close together. They borrowed, traded, and bartered with each other for goods and services. They also attended church services together and shared each other's burdens. "I'm so broke that they could sell me for a penny and get change back" was a common response to someone asking to borrow money from another sharecropper. These areas were usually identified by landmarks or structures close to their specific locations on the plantation. Arthur's family lived in one of eight houses located in the Shop Settlement, named so because of its proximity to the plantation's repair shop.

# 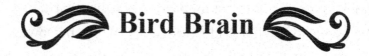 Bird Brain

Almost everybody on the Hobbs plantation had a nickname. The nicknames often were assigned based on a person's personality, appearance, or something else that was unique to them. Stump Jones and Stump Brown were short men, Slim Harris and Slim George were tall and skinny. The Boll Weevils were a family that could collectively pick large quantities of cotton. The six Kimble brothers, who were thought of as schemers working to trick people out of money, earned the nickname of Bushwhackers.

Arthur's Uncle Herman, expanded Arthur's occasional nickname of Bird which originated from his skinny legs to "Bird Brain." This nickname change occurred after Arthur went on a road trip with his Uncle Herman. The two had traveled about three miles from the Bird's home when Herman pulled his car to the side of the road and turned off the engine. He told Arthur he was going to visit one of his friends who lived in a house in the cotton field about 30 yards away from where they were parked. Herman asked Bird to throw a big rock to hit the house's tin roof if a brown Ford truck approached. He had his nephew to repeat his directions until he was satisfied that Bird would follow his instructions.

Herman left Bird in the car and went into the house. Since temperatures in the 90s made for an extremely hot and muggy day, Bird felt like his body was cooking inside his Uncle Herman's even hotter car. To cool off a bit, Bird decided to take a short walk. About 50 yards away from the car, he sat and relaxed under the shade of a big oak tree. Amid his vigilant watch, Bird fell asleep. The sound of a loud muffler woke him up as a brown Ford pickup truck sped past him and in the direction of Uncle Herman's parked car. Arthur jumped up and ran toward the car just as the truck stopped in the yard of the house his uncle was visiting. As the driver got out of his truck, Bird saw Herman run out of the back door of the house. A flying undershirt and then a cap followed Herman out the back door. Clutching his pants, Herman was butt-naked except for his boots as he ran through the cotton field toward his car. Herman and Arthur arrived at the car at almost the same time.

FATHERLESS

Herman was panting and nearly out of breath as he drove away while throwing his clothes onto the back seat. He shouted at Bird as he drove. "Boy, yo a dumb-assed boy, all I axed you ta do is throw a damn rock if ya saw a brown truck. Ya couldn't do dat! I thought da you had good sense, ya got bird legs, but ya ain't got da brains of a bird. Herman started calling his nephew "Bird Brain." The nickname stuck with him, but Arthur's daddy Otis changed the nickname back to Bird.

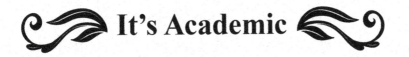

# It's Academic

School attendance was not mandatory. This explained the big yellow school bus making stops throughout the Hobbs plantation and leaving the community as empty as it was when it arrived each school day morning. Blacks living on plantations barely earned enough to survive. Most of them could not read or write. To the contrary, the parents had higher educational aspirations for their children. Yet, a child who could pick a 100 pounds of cotton each day carried more immediate economic value to both the sharecropping family and the plantation owner than an academic achiever. Plantation owners exerted pressure on sharecropping families and other laborers to make sure all able bodies in their households worked the fields during cotton chopping and harvest times. To plantation owners like Junior Hobbs and others across the South, large families were more valuable to them than small ones. Cotton was king, therefore spring and fall saw high absentee rates for black children attending the county's segregated schools. Attendance was better during times when the cotton fields were too wet for tilling, planting, maintaining or harvesting.

Students in Bird's community were able to attend school until the age of 21, gaining a little extra time to catch up on some of the academic lessons missed while picking and chopping cotton. Social promotions did not exist. As a result, six- and seven-year-old children were often in the same grade with 17- and 18-year-old students. During the fall, classes began at 8: 00 a.m. and ended at noon. School age children arrived home from school just in time to spend a half day picking cotton.

Bird admitted he didn't know all he needed to learn, but he also knew he did not want to be like the fifth-grade student at Tucker Attendance Center who came to a school play. The student's girlfriend and three children were with him. The young father was committed to staying in school as much as possible to improve his reading, math and other skills, even if it meant attending the same school as his children.

Poverty abound, many of the children growing up on plantations like the one where Bird and his siblings lived seldom bathed, had breakfast, brushed their teeth, or combed their hair. When they managed to make it to school, their personal care and hygiene didn't see much of a change. Most came from a single parent household with the mother being the main bread winner. Husbands, fathers and male heads of household fled Mississippi for cities like Memphis, St. Louis, Gary, and Chicago. Humbling themselves to the often required "boy" status instead of the "man" God made them to be left many black men struggling with the choice of living to make another day, being sentenced to the Parchman Prison Farm to work for years just for being black or dying a death as Emmett Till. They were well aware of the high odds of being wrongly imprisoned, murdered and dumped in a river or lynched to become that "strange fruit hanging on a tree." Many of them fled the South in search of better financial opportunities and more progressive lifestyles for themselves and their families. Some just disappeared, never to be heard from again as their loved ones prayed they were somewhere alive and safe. Of course, other daddies just stayed and hid in plain sight as they attempted to avoid parental responsibilities as well as the strife of Jim Crow.

FATHERLESS

 **Gallows Humor**

Typically, prior to leaving home each weekday morning, Wilma Ann would awaken Arthur and his siblings. Always, she would mete out an assortment of premonitions, instructions and warnings. The morning that he seemed to frustrate his mother by asking her of the whereabouts of his daddy, Bird drifted in and out of awareness as if he were floating in and out of a hyperbolic tank. He was too sleepy to be scared and too scared to really sleep. He didn't know the reason, but he considered situations that might be troubling his mama. He pondered the recent times he disobeyed Wilma Ann. Could it be that she had discovered his indiscretion of the week? What if she knew about him and his friends slipping down to Mr. Sugar Bear's watermelon patch and eating melons until their bellies almost burst. They dug holes in the ground and buried the evidence of green rinds in the holes. Certainly, none of his friends would have confessed to the thievery because all of them had sworn a sacred oath to each other. Everybody crossed their hearts and hoped to die before they would tell anyone of their watermelon patch deeds.

Still drowsy and in and out of grogginess, Bird noticed his mama's face showed an abundance of sadness and pain. This vision caused a tingling, cramping sensation in Bird's head. Terrified and bewildered, Bird cried a strangled whisper, "Mama, my belly feels kinda funny." Although she glanced toward him, Wilma Ann did not respond to her son's complaint. Lying in bed, Bird dozed off again, but he was startled awake when he heard a faint voice calling his name. Wilma Ann's squeezing of his right arm brought him wide awake. "Boy, crazy-ass Hon is out dir blowing lack truck horns goin outta style. I got ta go fore dat black no count bastard make me hafta cut him from asshole to appetite. The worse thang dat drunk peckerwood Junior ever did wuz ta git Hon a truck an let him start hauling field hands ta werk. Dere is sum cornbread n salt meat on der stove fer you ta eat. Feed yore sister 'n brother, stay in da yard. If'n I heah dat you played in dat road, I'm gon beat you lack you broke in da Beulah bank n didn't git no money," ranted Wilma Ann.

As she moved away from Arthur and Otha's bed. Quietly, Wilma Ann wrapped a small towel around her equalizer--an ice pick--and tucked the trusty weapon inside her bra. As Bird silently prayed his mother would not get in any fights that day, Wilma Ann shuffled out the front door. It slammed so hard that the walls of the entire little shotgun house shook. Secured under one of her arms was the brown paper bag containing her breakfast and lunch as Wilma Ann swung her other arm as if it were propelling her forward to Hon's borrowed truck.

Wilma Ann climbed on the back of the 1950 black Chevy pickup truck. Ruminating about whatever was going on with her and Otis, she told herself that she was going to have to be both mama and daddy to their children. She would try to make it by getting a remedy for her aching heart. She would also request Ms. Dinky Mae Banks, the plantation healer, to conjure up a financial blessing to help get her and the kids through the winter. If Ms. Dinky's fix worked, Wilma Ann calculated that she would have a good shot at trying to make life for her and her children work out without Otis. After all, Ms. Dinky understood how to take evil omens and spells off sufferers. Rumors throughout the plantation proclaimed she had to be good because she wore a cat's paw attached to a small chain around her neck and a three-legged cat roams happily around her house.

FATHERLESS

Most of the field hands who rode to the fields attempted to nap until they arrived at work. Monk Jones was sitting beside Lucy's Brown's big mouth son. People called him Copy Tack. He was always talking, never shutting his mouth. As usual, Little Leg Pearl was feverishly fluttering her long eyelashes at Copy Tack. Both, Cripple Jake and Molly Jones were nodding off and trying to sleep. Billy Clayton was looking mean and frowning at everybody. People called him Lawman because he tried to imitate Marshall Dan Troop from the western television series. His mama Bertha sat beside him. The right side of the truck was empty. The most coveted seats on the bench adjacent to the back window of the pickup already had two people sitting on it. It was the favored seat area because it had the best view and only two to three people could fit in the area.

"Hi yawl 'all done," asked Wilma Ann. "Fine," responded almost everyone in unison. Often, impoverished blacks made their lives more tolerable through this ribbing each other via a satire known as "gallows humor." This meant laughing at many of their own situations, flaws, worries, mannerisms, and quirks. Wilma Ann stuffed herself onto the window seat between nosey Rosie Metcalf who was chewing on the last of some buffalo fish and "Miss Know It All"

Charlotte Brown who kept a small Styrofoam cup in her hand as a spittoon for the snuff she dipped. Both were also large women who usually got hot and mad at or about almost any and everything. Everyone knew that they were about to be entertained when they saw Wilma Ann that morning. Wilma Ann eagerly hoped that the constant chitchat back and forth between herself other field hands would distract her from her Otis problems. She needed to get her mind off her troubles for a little while. The crew onboard was already prepared to rib themselves and each other. Wilma Ann dived right in.

"Rosie, wuz dat piece of fish ever alive?" asked Wilma Ann. "If ya had de sense dat God gave a coon, you would know dat dis is fresh fish, as big as yo nose is ya should smell dat," Rosie replied. Wilma Ann was about to respond when Lucy Brown nodded her head in agreement with Rosie. "Lucy, ya need ta tell yo liddle fast tail gal ta stop grinning at every boy she sees. Dat ole roguish, no count boy uh Minnie Pearl been eyeballing her," Rosie continued. "Preciate it, I shore will, I done tole her dat a hard head make a soft arse. I'm gon beat da faseness outta her," Lucy said.

Then, Wilma Ann shouted in Hon's direction, "Ya packed us tagether lack sardines, somebody breakin win an it smell lack somethin crawled up in dem n died. I

FATHERLESS

hope nobody lights a match! We might all blow up n soma yawl gon be in hell fore da devil git da news."

The sounds of laughter reverberated from the back of Hon's truck. Hon was not amused. Wilma Ann may have been "shooting the bull" about riders passing gas, but Hon knew the foul smells in and around the truck would be getting worse as more field hands piled on to the truck. Adding to his apparent foul mood was the fact that he had not had his morning coffee and still had several more stops to make as he anticipated somebody not being ready to go whenever he arrived in front of their house.

Foul scents usually filling the air around the field hands in the semi-closed space came from more than flatulence. There were various causes that ranged from rotted teeth, putrid breath, lye soap and plain old stinky, musty, funky, sweating body odor. Most field hands washed up every night, but baths were reserved for Saturdays when they had more free time than they had on working from sunrise to sunset weekdays. Wilma Ann often referred to her weekday work hours in the cottonfield as "working from can't see" (in the morning) to "can't see" (in the evening). Getting out of the fields by noon Saturdays gave field hands a little time to relax, bathe and generally take care of themselves and their children. Consequently, the weekday washups didn't take care of the body odors for any length of time. Furthermore, workers didn't always wear clean clothes to the fields and the baking soda used as deodorant was not very dependable. They wouldn't put perfume and cologne fragrances on weekday bodies. Those aromas were reserved for juke joints and church.

Yet, the smell of field hands in the morning was mild compared to any whiff of them after 12 hot hours of hard labor in direct sun. The laboring included constant contact with cotton poison, worms, lizards, frogs, and even snakes! Wilma Ann and her co-workers crushed, hit, evaded, and knocked down many other creatures as part of their cotton chopping and cotton-picking duties. (...and years later, a good number of field hands on Hobbs plantation and across the South succumbed to cancer caused by their constant contact with poisonous pesticides sprayed on the cotton and oftentimes sprayed on them while they were working in the cottonfields.)

Just as water at the homes of sharecroppers was a precious commodity for daily cooking and a weekly bath, water in the cotton fields, water was as precious. It was primarily for drinking and preventing dehydration of the field hands. A water boy brought a pail of cool water to workers about once every two hours. If the water boy's pail of water became empty, those workers farther along into the field may find themselves about to faint by the time they received water.

Water was considered too valuable to use for handwashing. Field hands ate their lunch with dusted off, still dirty hands. There were no toilets or outhouses in or near the cotton fields. When workers needed to relieve themselves, they did so by "going to the bushes." Laborers used tall cotton and grass for cover and small pieces of cotton as tissue to wipe their private areas.

Picking cotton involved pulling the cotton out of cotton bulbs and putting it in a sack that was 10 feet long. The sack was dragged forward between cotton rows by the person picking cotton with the sack's strap hung across their neck and shoulder. Toward the end of each day, as the sun dropped over the horizon, the temperatures cooled and laborers began to look toward the freedom of the evening as they headed to collect $2.50 per 100 pounds of cotton in their sacks. Some earned a dollar. Others picked enough to get a few more dollars. Wilma Ann collected as much as $10. As Hon halted the packed truck at the edge of a sea of cotton stalks brimming over with opened bolls of fluffy white cotton, workers jumped out. They grabbed long empty canvas sacks and headed to an open row to begin their work.  Wilma Ann was methodical in her work, simultaneously picking cotton from both a row on her left and on her right. As some of the workers wondered how much cotton they would pick each day, Wilma Ann had a goal that she knew she had to meet in order to keep a roof over her children's heads--400 pounds a day!

# 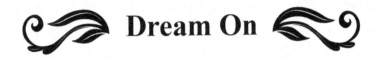 Dream On

Bird was dreaming again. He thought that his daddy had awakened him sometime before daybreak and told him that he had to leave. In the dream, Otis would not tell his son when he would return. Groggily in and out of a dream state, Bird saw himself surrounded by fire inside a huge fireplace. Bird couldn't find a way to escape the hot flames and it seemed as if someone kept adding more wood onto the fire. Bird woke up from his hallucinations very frantic and sweaty. His devastating nightmare came to an end and he stirred awake around eight o'clock that morning. The sun had beaded down on the tin roof for two hours and increased the temperature inside the house to a hotness that made Bird feel like he was having a heat stroke. He glanced at the unscreened windows. They were nailed shut primarily to keep out snakes. A breeze from the windows was not going to happen. Tightly shut windows combined with the heat of the hot tin roof made the shotgun house unbearable to be in during daylight of the summer and fall seasons. Since most teenagers went to work in the fields with their parents, the younger children like Bird, Otha and Mae were largely unsupervised throughout the work day. Older children who were eight, nine, 10 and sometimes 11 years old oversaw their younger siblings. With their parents and older siblings working in the fields, Bird and the other children mainly sought a good meal and then, just have some fun.

Traditionally, children gathered for play according to their age and gender. By the time Bird woke up from his nightmare, his sister and brother were already outside on the porch. Bird checked the breakfast Wilma Ann had prepared and left for them. He gathered some hotcakes and salt meat off the stove onto a plate and shared the food with Otha and Mae. He told them to stay on the porch of their house while he walked the quarter mile distance to the repair shop where his daddy worked. Several men on Hobbs plantation drove tractors. Some drove and operated huge cotton strippers, combines and other machines to comb and vacuum up the cotton before emptying it into a long trailer box and prepare the cotton for the cotton gin. At the gin, cotton was separated from its seeds. A few men like Bird's daddy regularly worked in the plantation machine repair shop.

FATHERLESS

Mr. Jack, the first person Bird saw on his visit to the machine repair shop, sometimes worked with Otis. "Hey, Mr. Jack," said Bird. Mr. Jack nodded in Bird's direction, but he did not make eye contact or verbally respond. "Is my daddy in the back?" asked Bird. Mr. Jack was ordinarily very jovial, but there was a sadness on his face as he put his arm on Bird's shoulder and said, "Son, ya need to ax your mama bout Otis. He ain't werking today. Now, ya gon back home an be careful dat ya don't git run over by a car."

Bird was troubled and uncertain on his return walk home. Then, like a light bulb going off in his brain, Bird concluded that his daddy must be visiting somebody, or maybe he went to check on another job. Surely, Otis would come back home that evening, the young boy thought as he came closer to their home. Several of his friends had huddled on the highway near Bird's house. As he drew near to them, Bird saw four pickup trucks and men unloading furniture into a house just a short distance down the road. Before he could ask what was going on, one of the boys told Bird that John Newman's relatives, whose home on the Mississippi River levee had floated away in a flood, were going to be staying in John's old house. Also, John, his parents and his siblings had all moved to a different plantation.

FATHERLESS

Bird did not know these people and he was going to ask a few questions about the new family and the fire. However, his fact-finding mission was halted when several of his friends started laughing and playing the dozens. After they told jokes and trash-talked each other's mothers, June Bug was declared winner of the dozen's contest. He told Hook Foot that his mama could put her face in some dough and make monkey cookies. The group roared with laughter. Suddenly, a hush replaced the laughter when the most beautiful girl in the world stepped out of the front door of the house where the line of trucks had men unloading furniture. The beautiful girl was about the same age as Bird and his friends, but she seemed to float as she walked. Bird's friend Hank had a big gap between his two front teeth that caused him to drool whenever he became too excited. Spit started to fly from Hank's mouth as other boys quickly moved away from him. Bird left his friends hob-knobbing and grabbed a chair off the truck. He took it into his new neighbor's house. Curious to see if the girl's daddy was one of the men unloading furniture, Bird turned to see all of his friends grabbing small items to bring into the house, too!

A man whom Bird assumed was the girl's daddy thanked Bird and the other boys as the pretty girl sat in

FATHERLESS

a chair on the front porch and nodded her approval at the boys. Bird decided right then and there that he might marry this girl. However, with all the competition, he knew he needed to "woo" her first. His older sister's boyfriend Roy termed the process of getting a girl's attention as "wooing" Roy told Bird that it was a way to get a girl's attention.

Bird went home, washed his face and under his arms. He oiled his face and hair with the green Royal Crown grease. Then, he donned his black church suit, black bowtie, white shirt and black shoes. Before he strolled out the front door, Bird recalled seeing a boy in a magazine wearing a suit and showing off an extra pair of different colored pants across his arm. Bird's church suit only had one pair of pants, but Bird grabbed a pair of his jeans and folded them over his right arm. He was ready to "woo" the pretty girl on the porch. As soon as Bird walked out of his house, some of his friends who saw him dressed up started laughing. Bird was undeterred, he asked the pretty girl her name. "Coolly Mae Brown," she replied. Coolly started grinning and saying, "Great green gobs of greasy, grimy gopher guts, contaminated monkey meat and amputated chicken feet stirred up n the pink lemonade without a spoon." It was a strange nursery rhyme or maybe an early version of rap, but it sounded like some black magic voodoo to Bird. In that moment, Bird quickly decided that he was not going to "woo" Coolly anymore.

Dejected, Bird started back home. He saw Miss Addler Boxer standing in front of his house. She had a justly earned reputation as the nosiest person on the Hobbs plantation. The 80-year-old gossiped so much that she often repeated the same rumors five or six times to several of the same people. Thanks to Junior, Miss Addler did not have to work in the cotton fields or even pay for things she got at the plantation store. A few years earlier, Junior was on one of his drunken sprees. He claimed he was going "blackbird" hunting in a densely wooded area. Pearly Williams, Junior's late-night "nurse," rode in the truck with Junior. As Junior shot his gun in the air, Pearly screamed while running toward Junior. Junior started shouting at Pearly, "Hellfire, I didn't mean ta kill her, I thought she was a deer." Pearly was trying to console Junior as his victim, Miss Addler, limped on a bleeding leg toward the two of them. Miss Addler persuaded Junior and Pearly that she would be okay as she tore the hem of her dress and wrapped the flesh wound on her leg. She told Junior and Pearly that she would "shore hate fer" Junior's wife or Pearl's husband, who was about to complete his five-year prison sentence, to "heah bout"

FATHERLESS

Pearly and Junior's late night rendezvous in the woods. After that day, Miss Addler was unable to work due to her "injuries." As a sort of worker's compensation, she kept her row house among the sharecroppers on the Hobbs plantation. Junior let her have it rent-free! Although Mrs. Hobbs, Junior's wife, did learned of her husband's blackbird hunting indiscretion with Pearly, she went a step further to appease Miss Addler in exchange for her continued silence. Junior's wife provided Miss Adder a free grocery account at the plantation store.

Miss Addler noticed Bird slumping about after the other kids had laughed and jeered at him when Coolly apparently rejected him and spouted off some weird verse too deep or too stupid for Bird's understanding. Miss Addler growled, "Come heah boy! Yo mama gon whup yore hind pot bout playin in yo church clothes. Git in da house and pull um off now!" Bird obeyed her orders and went inside their home to change clothes. He tried to stay inside until Miss Addler walked on down the road. When Bird came back outside, all his friends--along with Mr. Brown, Coolly and everyone who was in the new neighbor's house earlier--had disappeared.

Sundown was upon the Delta and few automobiles were traveling Highway 447. The time had arrived for Bird to make sure his younger sister and brother were

FATHERLESS

secure near the front porch of their house. Their mama was due to come home at any moment, causing Bird to look up the highway several times. Instead of seeing the field hand truck with Wilma Ann in route, Bird thought he saw his dad trying to get out of a blue car. Then, he thought he saw a tractor coming down the highway but turning away from their house. Realizing he was losing focus or "seeing things," Bird decided to forget about Wilma Ann and his siblings so he could enjoy "the cool of the day" and marvel at the disappearance of the sun as the big orange sphere seem to "kiss" the far western edge of the cotton field. He had one of those moments where his mind wandered. He was pondering where the sun went as it disappeared over the horizon. The sound of Hon's borrowed truck swiftly approaching pulled Bird from his stupor.

"Boy," ya been acting good?" Hon asked as he glared at Bird. "Yes sir," answered Bird. Wilma Ann slowly climbed from the back of the truck. "Don't let da doe knob hit cha whar de good Lawd split ya," someone in the truck shouted as Wilma Ann walked into the house. Bird glanced toward the shop where his dad normally worked as Wilma Ann told him and his siblings (who had suddenly appeared on the porch) to come inside the house. She said, "Arthur, you, Mae, and Otha set on my bed." Bird felt a knot in his throat, every time his mama used that expression, unwelcomed news always followed. Wilma Ann picked up one of Otis' old belts, looked at Bird, and shaking her head, went outside and sat on the steps at their backdoor. She was sobbing loudly with her face in her hands.

Although, Wilma Ann had not said anything to her children about Otis not coming home, Bird and his siblings realized something was seriously wrong with their mother and that their dad's absence would create a major void in their family. As each day passed without his dad, Bird felt the aching hole in his heart consuming him. All of them were sorely missing Otis. His absence unsettled Wilma Ann, but Bird's enchantment with and love for his daddy created a desperate change in him. Every night during the first week of Otis' absence, Bird tried to go to sleep early and unsuccessfully sought sound peacefulness and real rest. He persuaded himself that his daddy would be home when he awoke. His belief was so strong that he was upset and sad when Otis was not home on mornings following his restless sleep. When he did not see his daddy, Bird decided the only logical conclusion was his daddy must have come back while he was asleep and left before he awoke. Many times, while fitfully sleeping, Bird dreamed he heard his daddy saying, "Is that right?" That was his dad's usual response when expressing doubt about something.

FATHERLESS

 Otis

For two weeks straight, every weekday morning after his mama left to pick cotton, Bird would stand on the highway and look for his daddy. More days passed without any word from Otis. The constant pain on his mama's face continued to concerned Bird. His parents taught their children to keep their troubles to themselves and his daddy's philosophy was "whether you have a $100 or not a penny to your name. you better look the same as if you had a $100 every time you walk out of your house." Bird's imagination went into overdrive. He lost interest in playing and exploring the woods near his house. He became quiet and withdrawn. Bird concluded that given enough time, he could figure out where his daddy went.

Bird started to having mild hallucinations to the point of every black man he saw resembled his daddy. He heard his daddy calling him, only to discover that he had imagined hearing his dad. Bird wondered if his daddy was under the house and would not come out. Surely Otis heard his son begging for him to come back home. Some days, Bird believed his daddy was probably on the airplane that was spraying poison on the cotton in the fields surrounding them. When the plane landed, his dad would get out of the plane and make his way home. After all, they had much to discuss. Bird's daydreaming continued. As time passed, Bird found himself worrying less.

One Saturday morning, Bird's mother came into her children's room to wake all of them. "Everybody git up! We movin," shouted Wilma Ann. Bird dressed as fast as he could, guessing that his daddy had finally come home to get them. However, Bird's heart dropped when he saw Mr. Heely Fox back his pickup truck to the front door of their house. Wilma Ann ordered Mr. Heely to take a load of furniture to the new place. She told Bird to make sure that he, Otha and Mae don't move from the front porch until she returned for them. More truckloads of goods and furniture and several hours later, Wilma Ann showed her children the sharpshooter house that was now their home. It was located down a10-mile dusty rock lane called Easter Road. Barely wide enough for one vehicle to pass another, Easter Road was named for Harry and Beth Easter. They were owners of the plantation where Wilma Ann moved into another white-washed, wood-framed, three-room house. Further securing the plantation's theme name, every Easter morning, Beth Easter would have her chauffeur deliver big bags of colorful boiled and candied Easter eggs along with fruits and small toys to each sharecropper's residence located on their farm.

Although Bird missed his buddies on the Hobbs plantation, the move to Easter Road was a much-desired change by Wilma Ann and her children. In no time, Bird became quick friends with nearby boys from the Brown and the Leaks families. Bird's maternal grandparents, three aunts, including Aunt Big Sis and several cousins also lived along Easter Road. Being around his extended family improved Bird's mood. However, Bird couldn't help his constant focus on the need to find his dad. Increasingly frustrated at her son's persistent questions about locating Otis, Wilma Ann finally stressed to Bird, "Yo daddy walked off and left alla of us. If n he wuz coming back, he would be back by now." Bird replied, "How would Otis know how to find us because we moved, and his car probably broke down when he was looking for us. Daddy may be trying to get some gas for his car, and it has a flat tire." Bird imagined Otis went to their previous house and was waiting for his family to come back home. He decided his mother just didn't understand, therefore he would have to meet Otis and show him where they now lived on the Easter plantation.

Wilma Ann finally broke her silence about Otis coming back. She spouted a hodge-podge of her own logic, including the concept that her eldest son must be "half crazy" to expect Otis to come back for them. His daddy had gotten her pregnant three times and he had left her after each pregnancy, she reminded herself as she exploded in sharing the long-held information with Bird. In her opinion, Otis' departure from his family this time was no different than his previous disappearances. She continued to encouraged Bird to forget about his daddy because, obviously, his daddy had forgotten about him. Wilma Ann reminded her son that she was now both the mama and daddy! She insisted that the best thing for Bird to do was to stop his whining because "his no-good daddy had not even sent him a soda cracker to eat!"

As he reflected on his mama's attitude, Bird concluded Wilma Ann must have said something terrible to his daddy--making Otis mad enough to abandon his family. In Bird's opinion, his mom always talked too much and, anyway, he wondered why people liked her so much. His daddy spent a lot of time with him and took his children for a ride every Sunday. To Bird, Otis was the smartest, best dressed, most significant, towering and handsome man in the Delta. Bird swelled with pride when he heard many of his neighbors boast about his good looking and sharply dressed daddy and how Otis always looked Mr. Junior Hobbs directly in the eyes when they talked. Junior never referred to Otis as "boy," in the customary way that most Southern whites addressed black men. Otis had the rare fortune of being one of the few plantation tenants to own a car. He was a big man, standing six feet and two inches tall and weighing 250 pounds. He was intelligent, could read and write and was the go-to man for many sharecroppers requesting him to interpret, explain, or complete documents for them. The Tennessee native move to Bolivar County, Mississippi, with his mama and new stepdaddy when Otis was just out of the eighth grade.

Despite Otis' best laid plans, at the young age of 28, he had a common law wife, one stepdaughter who hated him and three children of his own with Wilma Ann. He never intended to be a country boy, tractor driver, mechanic or field hand. With the exception of his family, Otis had little love for living in the Mississippi Delta. He detested its endless fields of cotton, rice and soybeans. He hated the region's intense summer heat that was intensified due to the clearing of many trees, bushes, and other types of vegetation to make way for the mass cultivation of cotton, soybeans, rice and other crops. As if he were Satan on a throne of hellfire, Otis condemned the Delta's constant dust, country foods and the lack of cultural enrichment and entertainment available for a young man as himself.

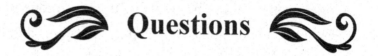 **Questions**

Bird asked his Aunt Big Sis to tell his daddy if he comes back home, he would build a tree house for the two of them to live in so they could be away from Wilma Ann and Otis would never have to leave again. Aunt Big Sis nodded to Bird as he continued. She was always willing to listen to the starry-eyed enchanted child and to provide her brand of wisdom to him and anyone else who. Unlike her siblings, who had many children, Aunt Big Sis had only one child. Other family members often referred to her son as "spoiled rotten." Bird felt his Aunt Big Sis just liked children and him in particular. She often treated him like he was her own son, too.

"Did my daddy come by your house?" Bird asked Aunt Big Sis. "If Otis' come by here, we wuz probably sleep. He did not knock on the front door loud enough to wake us up." she said with a smile.

FATHERLESS

"He probably went somewhere looking for a better job so he could buy ya lots of toys for Christmas. When he comes by here, I will be shore ta tell him that you need ta see him before he goes ta the store ta buy your toys. Now tell me three toys dat you won't ya daddy or Santie Claus ta git ya," she said. Bird quickly responded, "BB gun and a bicycle!"

Aunt Big Sis lived in the first house across the railroad tracks from Highway to 447, about a half mile south of the Town of Buffer. Bird knew that his aunt would keep her word and he figured his daddy had to pass by her house when he comes back to their current home on the Easter plantation. However, Bird felt he could not afford to take any chances. Every day except Sunday, Bird would trek up to Highway to 447, stand on the railroad tracks and carefully stare at every person inside the passing vehicles. He believed he saw his dad many times and to his dismay, Otis was always prevented from getting out of the car. Bird rationalized that his daddy could not free himself from the automobiles because the stops were to brief and the cars about were going too fast. Bird considered that Otis was smart enough to wait until the traffic slowed. In Bird's mind, as the cars reduced their speed, they were very likely to be on a road that Otis did not remember.

It would take some time for Otis to find his way back to their little town, considered Bird as his mind continued to wander in and out of logic and reasoning.

When Bird returned home from his "Otis watch," he was very sleepy, quite tired and aching from an ongoing daily pain in his stomach. He knew the stomach was from the lye he and his younger sister had mistakenly eaten. His sister's mouth appeared to turn inside out. She screamed as their parents rushed her to the doctor's house. Bird didn't know what medications the doctor gave her to ease her pain, but he decided it would be best for him to not tell anyone that he had eaten some of the lye, too. Instead, Bird decided to take his chances with the lye tearing up his stomach in lieu of Wilma Ann or Otis whipping his behind. Long after Otis left, Bird's stomach pain continued to be so severe at times that he was only able to walk bent over. As the pains progressively worsen, Bird trained himself to ignore them as much as possible because he could not let anything interfere with his focus to help his dad get back home.

#  God

Bird was elated when a commercial bus started operating along Highway to 447. He was confident the bus driver would allow his daddy to get off at Aunt Big Sis' house. He memorized the bus schedule and began getting to the railroad track about five minutes before the bus arrived. In case his dad accidentally got off a short distance away from Aunt Big Sis's house, Bird wanted to meet his daddy and show him the way to their home. The bus seemed to speed up as it passed the area where Bird was usually standing. It became obvious to Bird that the bus driver, who always waved at him, was part of a terrible scheme to keep his daddy on the bus. Bird was distraught about his daddy's troubles. He had tried to flag down the bus, so that he could get on and help his daddy fight his way off. However, the bus driver still would not stop. The driver slowed down and blew his horn at Bird as he drove by. Almost everybody on the bus gazed at Bird, waved their hands and smiled at Bird.

Eventually, Wilma Ann discovered Bird's trips to the railroad track. She grabbed him by the collar of his shirt and jerked him close to her. She pulled his face very close to hers and said, "If I catch yo liddle butt near dat highway again, I'm gon beat the black offa ya. Ya could git kilt trying to flag down a bus. I'd ruther hammer ya ta death myself den ta to have you splattered all over de road, cause ya got pancaked by a bus."

Bird accepted the fact that he would have to quit trying to stop the bus until he found out who told his mama on him. Bird had not yet started school and he did not know how to read or write; however, he drew a lot. He hatched a plan to draw figures that telling his dad what he wanted to say and put them in the mailbox in front of his house. Surely, the mailman would get his drawings to his daddy, Bird thought.

Bird drew pictures almost every day and put them in the mailbox in front of his house. Several times, he saw the mail man grin and take the drawings with him. After he used up all the scraps of paper that he could find, Bird drew on small pieces of wood and any other pliable item that he could get.

Bird awoke one morning in severe pain. His Mama was yelling as she whipped him with some long triple plaited willow switches. "Boy, if I catch ya near a mailbox fore ya git 40 years old, I'm gon take ya over da levee an feed ya ta da hongry alligators. "Da mailman seys he wuz gon ta haffa put ya in chains an take ya ta jail if ya ever go near dat mailbox agin," asserted Wilma Ann while giving Bird about 15 licks before tiring.

A few weeks later, Bird decided it was time to make one last attempt to stop the bus. He thought they might have to go and get his daddy, but he planned to be back home the next week. His mama was going to be very mad, but his daddy was not going to let her whip him or feed him to alligators. Bird drew some pictures on a brown paper bag telling Wilma Ann where he was going. He hurried to the highway without anyone from the plantation knowing. Bird stood in the middle of the road to make sure the bus driver would see him. The bus came closer and closer to Bird and the driver started blaring his horn as he slowed down and eventually stopped the bus.

Mission accomplished, Bird confidently stepped up to the door of the bus and held up a quarter to show the driver that he could pay his fare, Bird prepared to board the bus.

The driver opened the door, Bird placed his foot on the lowest step of the bus to board it. He was surprised at the height and size of the steps. After, he had both feet on the first step, a big, white man with red hair stood up from the driver's seat and blocked Bird's path. "What is your name?" he asked Bird. Bird replied, "Arthur, and I won't you ta let my daddy offa this bus!"

"Is that why I always see you standing on the railroad tracks when I drive by here? You have become very popular. The word has gotten around among our drivers and passengers about you watching our buses from the railroad track. Because of you, this route is widely discussed. Many of our passengers are puzzled about you. About your daddy--you remind me of myself when I was about your age. My daddy left me, too. It was years before I saw him again. I really missed him. Your daddy is not on this bus. I think I picked your daddy up right here. He told me to tell you that he is coming back soon, and your daddy wants you to be the man of the house until he gets back. He said he doesn't want you coming up to this highway anymore because he will probably get off the bus in Asher when he comes back. He does not want you to get run over before he gets back," the bus driver explained to Bird.

"Would you tell him we moved n he kin ax Auntie Big Sis ta point him to our house," Bird pleaded. "I sure will," said the bus driver as he started closing the pneumatic

FATHERLESS

folding door and prepared to drive away.

Bird hopped off the steps of the bus and laughed all the way home. He was going to wait on his daddy to come back home. He hoped he could remember all the things he needed to tell him. Although he usually kept most private thoughts to himself, Bird was compelled to share the good news that the bus driver had told him with his mama. To Bird's dismay, Wilma Ann was not delighted. She gave him two punishments. One was for disregarding her admonition to not go back to the highway. He mama claimed the second punishment was for him lying on the bus driver. In her mind, no way would a bus driver say what her son had reported to her. Bird wondered why God didn't stop Wilma Ann and verify to her that he was telling the truth. She finished whipping Bird and went outside to lay his tired body in the tall cotton field across from his house. He cried and criticized God until he became extremely sleepy. His regular bedtime was eight o'clock, but he went to sleep right there among the cotton stalks around six o'clock that evening.

Bird was very nervous and excited for the next couple of days. His mama had become crueler, and he wondered if his daddy and mama would ever like each other again. Bird decided to talk to his Aunt Big Sis again because apparently God was not answering any of his questions. He was surprised to see Aunt Big Sis in front of his house. Maybe God is listening a little, he thought. She and Bird exchanged greetings and Bird asked her if she had ever seen God? She replied that no one has seen God, but people have seen his son Jesus and some of the angels. She said that she had seen God's achievements. Bird asked if God ever talked to her?

"Yep," replied Aunt Big Sis. "All da time, he talks ta ever body." Then, Aunt Big Sis asked Bird if he ever saw God's works or heard him?" "No mam, he won't let me see him working, and he won't talk ta me neither, and he won't tell me where my daddy is, and he won't let me go ta where he is, and he won't stop mama from being so mean," Bird answered. Aunt Big Sis smiled and gently placed both of her hands on Bird's shoulders. She told him she had never met a child like him and since he was trying so hard to find God, maybe God had already found him. She said God can take any form or shape and can talk to people through their thoughts. "Ya continue to be a good boy, and soon ya will find 'em. The Bible ain't got a lie in it. It seys, 'seek and ye shall see,'" she explained. Before Aunt Big Sis could finish her sentence, Bird heard a voice saying, "Good boy, you have finally heard me. I have been with you all the time, every time you cried, I saw you. I heard you, every time you called on me, I came to you. You

FATHERLESS

were looking for me in the clouds, but I also live inside of you when the hard times became unbearable; and there are many more such times ahead."

Thanks to his Aunt Big Sis and the reassuring voice of God, Bird remembered to find a quiet place to tell God about his troubles. Thankfully, each time, Bird felt God eased his pain.

One Saturday afternoon, Bird saw a man who resembled his daddy. Realizing the man was not Otis, Bird's gut-wrenching stomach pain returned with a fury. To have a confidential talk with God and calm his pain, Bird walk nearly four miles through the cotton fields and settled down at a quiet spot on the ground. His nerves started to relax as he started to conversate with the Lord. Bird sometimes argued and often got mad with God. He told God, "I don't know why you won't let me see my daddy." An assertive voice said, "Your daddy is coming back." Bird told God that he, his brother and his sister needed to see Otis quickly. In hopes of strengthening his supplication and prayer, Bird threw in a hail Mary, adding even his mama needed Otis to come back home. To this appeal, the voice did not answer. Bird became angrier and emphasized his patience and urgency as he pounded the ground saying he has been waiting since he was a little boy to hear from God with a possible answer and no young boy should be without his daddy. He further claimed if he were God, he would take care of small children and keep them from crying and suffering. Bird demanded that God should admit it if he did not know where Otis was staying.

As the evening sun began to set, Bird exhaled a deep breath that sounded like it was somewhere between hope and defeat. He didn't know if he was convincing God because God was not defending himself or responding in any kind of way anymore. As his discussion with God went on for what seemed like hours, Bird tried his pure common logic out on the Lord. When that failed, he attempted to elicit sympathy from the master of the universe. He tried promises of ethical conduct. In the end, Bird resorted back to rage. The angrier Bird became, the more he reprimanded God for having made him. He threatened to run away from home and never go to church when he grew up since God was not fair. "You let other children have their daddies, but not me," exclaimed Bird. From the young boy's point of view, as his pitiful big brown eyes stared skyward, God did not seem to be interested at all in his life as a fatherless child.

Just before calling an "amen" to his fervent prayer, Bird decided to ask God for a small, much easier favor. As Bird searched his mind for the right words to express his request, tears ran down his face so big and fast that he found he could not think of one more thing to say to God. Through intermittent convulsive loud snorts and his watershed of tears, Bird struggled to breath. Finally, Bird gave up, resolving that his eternity of tears and inability to mouth even a small favor from God was nobody's business but God and his. The urgent need to get back home before dark took over Bird's questioning thoughts of God really being in the sky as the ministers preached. Realizing the lateness of the day, Bird knew without a doubt that Wilma Ann would be waiting on him with a belt if nightfall caught him away from home.

#  Lye

Bird very carefully dried his eyes and wiped his face with the back of his hands before going inside their home. He was surprised to notice the debilitating stomach pain that had been with him almost every second since his daddy left seemed more tolerable. Suddenly, overcome with peace and calm, Bird immediately laid on the floor by his bed and fell asleep.

The next day, Bird set off for another long walk so that he could cry and think in privacy. He thought a great deal about love. He knew that he loved plenty of people, including his mama and daddy, although they didn't seem to like him. He supposed he could at least like Jesus if only Jesus would help him out. Bird imagined that he was going to have to do without his mama and daddy. After all, Bird felt he had given his daddy every chance to come home. Maybe, his mama was right the countless times she explicitly stressed, "Otis walked off from us and he is not coming back!"

Through all of his commiserating, Bird decided he needed to focus on plots to get even with God. Furthermore, he found he was no longer feeling so enchanted about Otis. More and more, he was beginning to dislike his daddy. While stretched out and cooling down on the front room floor of the three-room house, Bird heard a persistent knocking at the front door. "Bird, hurry up n come outside," shouted his friend Bug. Bug had the most wonderful news. His daddy and mama had a new device never seen by most of the folks living on Easter plantation--a television! Occasionally, Bird gained permission to watch television shows with Bug. This magical box of moving and talking pictures streaming inside of it was a very exhilarating experience. Typically, when Bird arrived at Bug's house, the room was full of chatter by Bug's entire family and many neighbors who crowded the small front room. Everyone was amazed and captivated as they watched television at every opportunity. The western series Maverick became Bird's favorite show. The title characters were a team of gambling brothers. Always well-dressed, they were smart, witty, strong and agile. They could ride, fight and shoot well and the Maverick Brothers had a lot of love for their daddy.

One night, Bird dreamt he was riding and shooting with the Maverick boys when his Uncle Sonny awakened him. The oldest of Wilma Ann's brothers, Uncle Sonny was huge and rough. His booming voice exposed Sonny's colorful personality and terrible memory for names. He had a nickname for everybody. "Hey, Moo, git offa yo butt and go wit me," he boomed while poking Bird's belly with a thick forefinger. As they headed out the door, Wilma Ann hollered, "Sonny, don't drive too fast."

As Sonny flopped onto the driver's seat of his blue and white Buick Roadmaster, the huge car tilted downward on the driver's side. Bird sat in the passenger seat and closed the car door. "Moo, let's catch some air," said the jovial Uncle Sonny to Bird as they zoomed at a speed of some 60 miles per hour down Easter Road. Sonny left a thick cloud of brown Mississippi Delta dust behind him as he turned off the dusty road onto the main highway. Once on the paved State Highway 447, Sonny proceeded at speeds exceeding 100 miles per hour on their ride to nowhere and back home to sharecroppers' row on the plantation. Bird enjoyed every minute.

FATHERLESS

 Crying Times

Wilma Ann forced Bird, his younger sister Mae, and his baby brother Otha to go church every Sunday. Retha, his older sister, got a reprieve from going with them since she was almost living fulltime with her recently widowed Godmother to help her through her mourning period.

Wilma Ann said that the "Lawd" chose her to do his work. She believed He anointed her with special powers and grace to "make shore dat people straighten up an fly right." When she attended church, Wilma Ann hooped, hollered, cried and generally embarrassed Bird. Furthermore, Bird doubted her claims because he certainly was not having any personal contact with God, nor had anyone he'd spoken to seen God. Bird saw pictures of Jesus on walls in almost every house he lived in or visited. The Savior looked different in nearly every photo. One day after church services, Bird asked the preacher, "Is Jesus white or colored?" The preacher pulled him aside and explained that Jesus was a Jew and he had hair like wool. "Then who are the men on the pictures claiming to be Jesus," asked Bird.

The preacher explained, "Somethangs ya will learn by and by." Reluctantly, the next Sunday, Bird was back in church. The preacher was too excited, he talked too long, and it was too hot in the church. Women fainted all over the church and Bird was very uncomfortable. Yet, this Sunday was going to be very different for Bird. God was always supposed to be at the church. After all, church was God's house, according to the preacher and the grown people who went to church. They told everyone, "Call on him while he is near!"   Bird hoped he would see God before he left church that day.  God could get a message to Otis for him. He closed his eyes tightly, clenched his fists, and silently prayed, "Lord, dis is Arthur. I know dat I have not been good an I know dat I told my friend Bug dat you don't listen to children. You only lack grown folks. Still, if you let me see my daddy and stop mama from cussing and stuff, I will know dat you do hear an see little children. An I will tell my friends ta be good an ta say our father prayers

FATHERLESS

every night an ta say amen a lot. Don't forgit ta brang him home tamoro n don't let him git lost."

The next day, Bird was feeling optimistic that God would answer his prayers because there was still plenty of daylight. Suddenly, he remembered he forgot to be specific by telling God to bring his daddy back that morning, not leave his request open for Otis to return on any old day. A long time passed without a word from Otis or God. Bird boasted to some on his friends about his daddy coming back home. Several of them were stopping by Bird's house almost daily to see if his daddy had returned. Bird thought his buddies were the last people his daddy needed to see on his first day back home. As soon as he had the opportunity, Bird crawled under the house to think and be alone. It was a somewhat private space, despite the occasional frogs, dogs and crawling insects. The crawl space was dusty and dirty. Bird tried to steel himself to not cry, but the tears came flowing down his cheeks. As he tried to convince himself that he was not crying, his tears clouded his vision and hampered Bird's effort to crawl from under the house. Bird heard his friends calling his name. Since he didn't want them to see his face wet, Bird crawled farther under the house and big boys didn't cry unless they were at a funeral. The friends soon stopped calling for him and left. Bird crawled from his hiding place. He went on another long walk between the nearby tall rows of cotton to ponder why Otis didn't show up and why God didn't come through with answered prayers after his hours of passionate pleading and making promises to God.

 **Sweet Tobacco**

Some of the men who lived on Easter Road chewed tobacco. Overwhelmingly, their choice of brands was the "Bull of the Woods." After they purchased new packs of chewing tobacco, chunks of their old or stale tobacco were discarded. While on his way to visit his friends, Bird found a discarded package of old, partially used tobacco on the side of the road. He decided the free tobacco presented an excellent cost-free opportunity to start enjoying the chew of the Bull of the Woods as he had witnessed grown men doing. Although he would try the tobacco, Bird was confident the vice would be a temporary one for him since chewers spitting tobacco juice didn't really look cool.

Cool or not, many Mississippi Deltans smoked, dipped snuff, and/or chewed tobacco. Both genders and both blacks and whites seem to enjoy or be addicted to chewing tobacco or dipping snuff. Bird didn't understand what woes white folks had, but he had overheard talk that some blacks under the stress of poverty and constant racist Jim Crow harassment claim they found a little stress relief in the vice of tobacco chewing. Others added that a little gambling, drinking, sometimes fighting, and listening to blues music at local juke joints helped to keep their minds off the systemic oppression while trying to survive it. Apparently, while enjoying some relief on their way home from a juke joint, someone left Bird the gift of tobacco on the side of Easter Road.

Bird bit off a piece of the stale plug of pressed tobacco leaves. As he chewed, a sweet flavored liquid secreted in his mouth. Wondering why people spat the sweet juice of the tobacco out instead of swallowing it, Bird swallowed the tasty juice. Continuing his walked, the curve in the road seemed to be getting longer and longer. He sat down on the side of the side of the road to try to rest a bit. Hours later, Mr. Toot Bell, the oldest tractor driver on the Easter plantation, found Bird lying face down. Bird was happy someone was helping him get to his feet, but he regretted it was Mr. Toot. Grown folks regularly discussed the old man, saying, "If you want somebody to know something, you could telephone, telegraph, or tell Bell." Without a doubt, Bird feared his mama and everyone else

FATHERLESS

living on Easter plantation were going to hear about his chewing tobacco fiasco. Although he could barely hear or see, Bird noticed Toot chuckling. Then, Toot put his mouth close to Bird's left ear and shouted, "Wat's wrong wit ya, boy? Don't ya know it's over a hunerd degrees out here taday? What is dat brown stuff runnin out yo mouf an all-round yo nack? Have ya been dranking?"

Bird slurred an attempted answer. Toot smelled Bird's breath and began laughing out loud. "Tell ya wat I'm gon do boy. I'm gon give ya some cold water and gon go up ta de stoe. When I come back, ya better be done got rit of all dat tobacco an ya better be back at yo house. If ya don't be, I'm gon tell yo mama and she gon beat yo hind part so hard til ya gon have ta stand up the rest or yo life," he said between guffaws of laughter. Toot placed a large jar of water on the ground near Bird and drove away. Bird quickly drank all the water that Toot gave him and proceeded to stagger home unnoticed by anyone else. He made it home long before his mama returned from 12 hours of picking cotton. Thankfully, Mr. Toot kept his word. From then on, he and Bird acted as comrades with a special secret. Yet, Bird remained somewhat worried because Mr. Toot always seemed tempted to discuss the episode of him getting drunk on juicy tobacco.

FATHERLESS

# 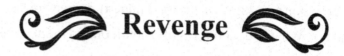 Revenge

With God's apparent refusal to fulfill Bird's desire to have his father return home, Bird decided he could get even with God by running away from home. He would do so the next Saturday morning while Wilma Ann was at the cotton field. Bird thought the Greyhound bus driver could drop him off at the same place where Otis got off the bus. Bird packed a pair of long drawers, an undershirt, a pair of clean jeans, a sweatshirt, and a washcloth into a pillowcase. Saturday morning came quickly. After his mama left home for her half day of picking cotton, Bird grabbed his packed pillowcase and prepared to leave. At the front door, he turned to look back through the house. Bird retreated. If he left home, his sister and brother would be alone. Just like that and despite all his planning, Bird made up his mind to stay with them for one more year.

A few nights later, Wilma Ann returned home very upset and clearly angry. Without explanation, she abruptly moved her family six miles away to the town of Grace. At the age of eight, Bird started first grade at Grace Elementary School. Aside from the fact that his daddy may not be able to find his family, Bird felt the move was a pleasant distraction from his troubled life. After all, for the first time in his life, he would be going to school! The reticent Bird rarely spoke to adults unless they said something to him. This was a rule, just like the "remember Emmett Till" mantra, that his mama had drilled into his head. The first-grade teacher, Ms. McKenny, placed the quiet Bird and seven other boys in a group at the back of the classroom. She designated the classroom tables A-F, attempting to group students at tables according to their learning capabilities. Ascertaining he could not read, spell, write his name, or count, Ms. McKenny placed Bird at the F table with three 16-year-old boys, two mentally disabled children, and a blind boy. The teacher spent most of her time with the children at the A, B and C tables.

Students sitting at the remaining three tables were generally ignored by Ms. McKenny. During the third week of school, she asked a question to which

FATHERLESS

Bird knew the answer. Instead of calling on Bird when he raised his hand, Ms. McKenny reprimanded him by saying, "Put your hand down! Tell your mama to get your hair cut. You looked like the wolf boy!" Bird did not know what the wolf boy was, but he did know that he did not appreciate the rest of the children laughing at him and calling him 'wolf boy.' When he told his mama what the teacher said to him, she replied that he couldn't let words hurt him. Many of the children who laughed had daddies who could take them to get their hair cut. She explained to Bird that she was barely making enough money to feed him and his siblings.

Bird walked uptown to Curly's Barber Shop and asked Curly about the price of a haircut. "Fifty cents," Curly laughed and added, "Come back to see me when ya git a little change in yo pocket." Bird could hear laughter filling the barbershop as he walked away. Taking matters into his own hands, Bird walked all over the Town of Grace. He searched for discarded empty Coke Cola bottles and sold his cache to Wingard Grocery for two cents a bottle. When he had saved 50 cents from his bottle sales, Bird returned to Curly's Barber Shop, paid the money, and received his first professional haircut.

FATHERLESS

As soon as Bird solved his haircut problem, another problem appeared. One of the 17-year-old boys who sat at the F table with Bird started bullying and beating him up. The eight-year-old Bird complained to Ms. McKenny about his nemesis, the class bully Charles Wilkes. She investigated Bird's claims, but Charles denied everything. Bird complained to his mama, but she did not believe him either because Charles had a reputation in the community as a friendly church-going boy. Without his daddy or any other adult to give him better advice or to stand up for him, Bird realized he had only himself to depend on to stop Charles. He remembered advice from his grandpa about how to fight from a point of strength when in a disadvantaged situation. The following weekend, Bird bagged a broad assortment of rocks and hid his ammunition in strategic areas across the school grounds. During recess the following Monday, as usual, Charles was walking around the rectangular-shaped school building looking for Bird.

Charles was heading around the northern corner of the school while Bird was standing behind Charles at the eastern edge of the building. Bird threw a big rock with the power and accuracy of Negro League baseball pitcher Satchel Paige. The rock hit Charles squarely in the center of his back! While Charles bent over in pain, Bird quietly slipped into the school and sat down with Ms. McKenney. Bird continued the same assault on Charles every school day until Charles became a nervous wreck. Bird did not reveal his anti-bullying campaign to anyone. No one else knew who or what was hitting Charles with rocks. Throughout the school day, Charles started jumping at all sudden noises. Consequently, the bully's mama thought it best to take Charles out of school so her son could rest for a week. Thanks to Bird's anti-bully strategic plan, when Charles returned to school, he was a "kinder, gentler person.

To the contrary, a lot of his own kindness was leaving as Bird felt increasingly alone in an unfriendly world. He found himself engaging in a fight almost every day. In fact, Bird decided that it was a waste of time to forgive people because people were going to take his forgiving them as a sign of weakness. He started keeping mental lists of negative things people said or did to him. One unkind way or another, Bird quickly got even with the younger people on his list. He fully intended to repay the older people back, too, when he got older.

There were a few young bullies at Grace Elementary School and most of them knew to evade

Bird. The exception was John Adams. Although John was the same age and size as Bird, John scared many of their classmates into giving him anything they had. He took their food, marbles and whatever else that they had and he wanted. One day, John had the audacity to grab Bird's neck with a chokehold, reach into Bird's pocket and confiscate Bird's prized and most beautiful marble. Customarily, at the time of a bully's attack on him, Bird did not retaliate immediately. Later that day, as he plotted his revenge, Bird decided the bodacious John needed something unique.

The best opportunity presented itself the next week when Ms. McKenny asked the two boys to replace a blown light bulb in her classroom. The room had a very high ceiling, John was the tallest boy in the class and Bird was the second tallest. When John volunteered, Bird immediately volunteered, too. To replace the light bulb, John stood on top of the back of a chair held by Bird. As John stood on his tippy toes and reached up to the ceiling, Bird jerked the chair from under his archenemy. After falling to the linoleum covered concrete floor, John was transported to Mound Bayou's Taborian Hospital for medical attention and healing. Bird was not so lucky. Ms. McKenny whipped him. The school principal followed with the school's approved brand of corporal punishment in the form of 12 licks with a thick leather strap. By the time Bird arrived home from school, Wilma Ann had already received word of his dastardly deed. She was waiting on him with an extension cord in her hand and a towel around her neck.

As she started in on her turn to whip Bird, she said, "Boy, ya almost kilt Ella's boy taday, and dat's what I'm gon do ta you! Pull off dat shirt. I don't wanna whup shirt, it didn't do anythang. I'm gon give you somethin that you gon tell yo grand chilluns about if ya live thru it." She proceeded to whipping Bird until his skin began to bleed. Wilma Ann took a 15-minute break and used the towel around her neck to wipe the sweat from her face, arms and hands. She drank a cold glass of ice water and started whacking Bird again. The bleeding Bird refused to cry as he wondered if he would ever live to be nine years old, let alone a grown man. Wilma Ann told one of the neighbor's children to go and get her some coal oil and a match. She said she was going to kill her son and be done with his iniquity.

By then, many of the neighbors learned of what was happening with Wilma Ann and her boy. Someone told the details to Reverend Brown who

FATHERLESS

quickly headed to Wilma Ann's house. Reverend Brown told her that she had whipped Bird enough. He said, "Ya bout to kill em." Wilma Ann replied that she intended to kill Bird. "But he's just a child," the preacher pleaded. Wilma Ann retorted that Bird was about to be a dead child. She continued to assert her rights to the preacher--explaining that she had brought Bird into the world and it was her time to take him out of it.

"Jesus said let he who is without sin cast the first stone. I know this boy. He gits a little mad when people mess wit him, but I never see him messing wit anybody first. He had no right ta do what he did, but you ain't got no right to try to kill him. Yo, daddy didn't kill you when you got mad and cut up yo sister's new dresses and set em on fire," continued Reverend Brown.

Wilma Ann responded that she didn't know anything about casting the first the stones because she had not yet hit Bird with any rocks. She reminded Reverend Brown that she had to be Bird's mama and daddy. The good Reverend responded, "I know, but ask yo self, would his daddy beat him like this if he was here? If he wouldn't, then you not being his daddy, you are being something else. I love ya in

Christ, but if you hit that boy one mo time today, I'm driving down to Able and brang yo daddy back up here, and he's gon do to you every thang you did ta that boy."

Wilma Ann took a deep breath and exclaimed, "I will not raise a gambler, a drunkard, a rogue, or a child dat wonts ta kill somebody!" Grudgingly, she decided she had whipped Bird enough for that day, however, she reminded Bird that she was going to whip him every day until Charles got well. Charles was discharged from the hospital the next day. Ms. Ella, Charles' mama, brought her son by Wilma Ann's house to apologize. She discovered that Charles had been beating up Bird and other little children. She asked Wilma Ann to have pity on Bird because Charles had promised God and anyone who would listen that he would never again bully anyone. His mama stated that Charles' fall on his head "thumped some sense into him."

The teachers and principal at Grace Elementary were not so forgiving. They watched Bird like a bunch of hawks eyeing a rat or snake. The educators reminded Bird daily that they were hoping he would "do anything to git what they had for him." After a week, Charles came back to school.

FATHERLESS

He and Bird became good friends. From time to time, Ms. McKenny slowly started allowing Bird to answer class questions. She grew to respect and be impressed with Bird's intelligence. By the end of the first semester, she promoted Bird all the way to the first table with the A students.

Before the school year ended, Bird was Grace Elementary School's top first grade student. Like adding whip cream topping to his mama's jelly cake, Bird also landed the lead part in the class play held to celebrate and mark end of the school year. Without a doubt in his mind, Bird finally felt like things were looking up in his life as he was promoted to the second grade.

#  The Field

Bird spent the summer picking cotton. He thought the work was fun because most of his classmates worked in the fields, too. The eight-year-old's favorite part of the workday was lunchtime, from noon to 1 p.m. At 11 a.m., the straw boss would write down orders of what each of the field hands wanted to eat for lunch. After collecting the lunch fare from everyone, the straw boss would drive to the nearest store to fill the orders. Excitement peaked as workers saw the straw boss and his pickup truck returning to the cotton field. Every cotton picker would rush to the truck to get their food and their change.

Bird usually ordered a cinnamon roll with icing, three pieces of chopped ham, some candied peanuts, a Baby Ruth candy bar and a bottle of Royal Crown Cola that was commonly known as a "belly washer." Bird liked to eat the chopped ham first to relish in the taste of its salty flavor. The cinnamon roll was next as Bird savored its sweet icing. The red burnt flavored candy-covered peanuts gave him a tasty semi-sweet crunch. As he sucked the chocolate covering off his Baby Ruth candy bar, Bird thought he finally had a taste of heaven. The next part of his lunch was highlighted with the naked sweet caramel of the Baby Ruth melting in his mouth. Lastly, Bird's lunch ritual was to put the peanuts and what was left of the caramel into the belly washer bottle of RC soft drink. The cola would sizzle as its acid melted the caramel and as the peanuts gently dropped to the bottom of the 16-ounce bottle. It was like watching art. Bird spent the remaining 15 minutes of the noon hour slowly drinking his cola and devouring his cola swollen peanuts.

None of the other children wanted to eat with Bird. They all agreed that he ate too slow. His mother, Wilma Ann did not like bread or sweets, but she loved all kinds of meat. She always ordered as much meat as she could afford and a cola. She gobbled her limited meal down within a few minutes and then took a short nap while Bird slowly reveled in the joy of every diverse taste and texture of his meal.

The second grade at Grace Elementary School seem to speed by. Many of the men in the Town of Grace took an interest in Bird's well-being and academic future. They were always reassuring and threatening Bird about the consequences of his actions. Some of them told Bird they were preparing to "beat the bark off him" if he hurt another child.

Ms. Wilkerson, Bird's third-grade teacher, gave him a peek at life outside the plantation when she required him to read a stack of magazines and discuss with her their contents. During the first month of the third grade, Bird was making good grades and he was beginning to be quite popular with teachers and students.

One day after school, Bird walked on the railroad tracks until he reached the short road leading to his house. As he came closer to their house, Bird noticed the curtains were gone from the windows. There was a truck parked in the front yard and a man standing alongside it. Bird walked up to the porch and the man asked, "Is you Ms. Wilma Ann's boy"?

"Yes, sir," Bird answered. "Yo mama axed me to brang yo wit me." Bird looked through the opened front door and saw that their shotgun house was empty. "Where is my mama, and what happened to our furniture" Bird skeptically asked. "She moved to Mr. Kudrow's place dis morning. It's bout three

FATHERLESS

miles from here and she told me to brang you to her,"
the stranger explained. The man seemed harmless,
therefore, Bird got in the truck. They headed to Mr.
Kudrow's place. which was apparently in the middle
of nowhere. Bird's next home was about two miles
from the main highway down a long dusty road. The
nearest house was about a mile and a half away, and
the closest child turned out to be about three miles
away. Bird tried to be optimistic, especially since this
was going to be the first time for him to ride a bus to
school.

The morning bus rides to Grace Elementary
School turned out to be quite entertaining. Boys were
always playing jokes and making a lot of noise. Also,
Bird loved to ride. Overall, he was feeling pretty
good.   One day, just out of the blue, upon returning
home from school, Bird's longing for the presence of
his daddy returned suddenly and hit him in his head
and heart like a stack of bricks!

 **Scared**

Once again Bird's thoughts returned to centering on his dad. Bird felt Wilma Ann was becoming more short-tempered and less thoughtful. She was always frustrated, and she generally took her disappointment out on Bird and his older sister, Retha. When their mother was not verbally abusing them, she was "in the streets," and sometimes for two days straight. Wilma Ann's absence was very frightening for Bird and his siblings, especially so considering that they lived far out in the country. At night, there were no lights except the single lamp they had in their house. When Wilma Ann stayed out all night, Bird and Retha were not able to get much sleep. Retha was a gorgeous teenager and men had started to lustily look at her. Bird became apprehensive for his sister's safety. Their door lock was only a bent nail attached to the door frame and twisted about two inches across the door's edge to secure the family from unwanted visitors. The children kept the single coal oil lamp lit and armed themselves with cast iron skillets as they sat with their backs against the fragile front door. They planned to fight to the death if anyone tried to break into the house. One night, about three hours after Wilma Ann left home, Bird and Retha heard loud footsteps crunching on the road near their home. As the sound of the footsteps landed on their front porch, the perpetrator stopped and became quiet.

Suddenly, a large black hand forced its way through the hole in their door where a lock had once been. Retha shouted to Bird, "Ya better hit wit all yo mite," as they used all their strength to crush the hand with a large black skillet and a piece of firewood. They heard a grunting noise from outside their door as the hand quickly yanked backward and escaped from the door hole. A series of strange groans continued, followed by the sound of rapid footsteps retreating from their porch. Shortly afterward, Bird and Retha heard the engine of an automobile roaring toward the main highway.

Less than a week later, an intruder attempted to break into their house by kicking in the front door. Bird and Retha stood ready to defend themselves. Retha shouted, "Dirty bastard, I know who you is. Break-

in here if ya wont ta, we got sumptun ready fer ya."
Retha must have been convincing because there was
a short silence, followed by the sound of footsteps
scurrying away from their house.

The attempted break-ins created a protective
bond between Bird, Mae, and Retha. At the same
time, these attempted violations of their safety almost
ruined the children's respect for many of the men
of the Mississippi Delta. Since Bird and his sisters
didn't know who the culprits were that tried to break
into their home, almost every man became a suspect.
Any man who smiled or seemed unusually kind to
them was an immediate threat.

FATHERLESS

#  Flashing Lights

The little peace Bird thought he might achieve while living on Kudrow's plantation was shattered when a loud humming tone that he had not heard before awoke him at four o'clock in the morning. He looked out of the front window where he saw way across the flat Delta land something resembling flashing Christmas lights moving South toward Bakersville, just about five miles from Bird's home. Bird's mama explained to him what he saw were swirling emergency lights of sirens flashing atop police cars.

Later that morning, when Bird arrived at school, teachers were talking about the cause of all the flashing lights Bird had seen the night before. From what Bird and the other children could gather from hearing the adults talk to each other, all the excitement was about the first black on black killing to occur in Bakersville in 20 years. Everyone seemed upset and generally impatient with each other. Nana Smith had been murdered!

Mamie and Abraham King were siblings. Nana Smith and Georgia Davis King were sisters. Abraham and Georgia were married. While the in-laws regularly argued, this time the argument became violent. Mamie stabbed Nana to death. The surrounding communities were in shock because of the rarity and savagery of the crime. The victim Nana was pregnant. Her unborn baby died, too. Most people in the area knew Nana, Mamie and their families. Wilma Ann cried for a week and she kept moaning, "It's a shame before God." As she continued mumbling unintelligibly phrases, she begged God to have mercy on everyone.

The anxiety heightened in around town and the nearby Grace where Bird and his family lived and sharecropped on Kudrow's farm. Wilma Ann became livid about Bob Wong not allowing her additional store credit. Wong directed Wilma Ann to a sign that he had recently brought and hung over the center of the counter. It read, "If you ask for credit, I no give you credit, you get mad. If you ask for credit, I give you credit, you no pay, I get mad. Better you get mad than me."

FATHERLESS

Bird's mama stormed out of the store, slipped and fell. The fall jolted her purse open, exposing all her standard self-protection arsenal--a 22-caliber pistol, a butcher knife and her trusty ice pick. Several onlookers watching from across the street laughed at Wilma Ann as she struggled to recover from the fall. Short and overweight, Wilma Ann ungracefully lifted herself to her hands and knees and on to her feet. One of the men walked across the street and helped steady her as she rose to stand. Wilma Ann turned, stared across the street at the persons who were laughing and declared she would have God curse them all for disrespecting her. The spectators laughed harder.

Wilma Ann closed her eyes, clenched her fist, bowed her head right there in the middle of the sidewalk and started her prayer. "Lord, yo know I'm, yo child. Ya always said dat if I called on ya in faith and truf and wit a sincere heart dat ya would fight my battles fer me. Lord, I'm axing ya ta put a cuss on all des ignant Negroes cross da street even dem dat did not laugh cause dey gon snicker when da git home. Lord, I don't won't ya ta kill nobody right now. But da need to be taught a lesson. So right now, jest brang up a bad stom and blow some sense into des crazy Negroes," she shouted.

As Wilma Ann finished talking, turbulence filled the sky. Thunder rumbled through the air. The sky became menacingly dark, and a mighty wind blew one of the street trash cans over and sent paper flying everywhere. The people who were standing outside began to run for cover. Wilma Ann walked a few steps before she tired. Stopping to rest, Wilma Ann and others noticed the rain, wind and thunder halted as suddenly as it had begun. The sun started to shine. Wilma Ann stood and bowed her head again as she loudly thanked the Lord "for showing ya power an da things dat ya will do fer saints lack running the no count Negroes offa de streets so decent people could go to the store!"

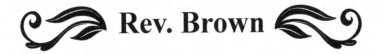 **Rev. Brown**

Despite his mother's comical and publicly embarrassing theatrics, Bird found his own current melancholy was not so much about Wilma Ann or Otis. He was sad and puzzled about God letting a baby "get killed." He needed to talk to Reverend Brown. Surely, if anyone had an answer, the preacher did. The good reverend always took time to teach things to children and he had certainly kept Wilma Ann from killing him. Bird was about to board the school bus when he spotted Reverend Brown. With permission from the bus driver Mr. Tinny Bee, Bird ran to talk to Reverend Brown. "Hey Sonny Boy, how you are doing?" asked Reverend Brown. "Fine, how bout you?" replied Bird. "I am blessed," answered Reverend Brown. "Reverend Brown, why did God let Nana's baby git killed, I thought he liked babies?" questioned Bird. "God loves everybody, even the girl that did the killing," the minister explained.

FATHERLESS

Bird asked Reverend Brown about several of his past sermons, especially the ones where he said folks who did terrible things are going to hell. Reverend Brown bent down to Bird's height and explained, "Nobody is bad in God's eyes, except the devil and his bunch. People sometimes do bad things. Everybody has done some wrong things, including me. I wuz a rascal when I wuz young and I'm so glad that God loved me and saved me when almost all my kinfolks gave up on me. I was on a fast track bound for hell. Ya see, sometimes good people do bad things, too. Nobody is perfect, but God is always ready to forgive people who ax him ta forgive them. Otherwise, we could not make it to heaven. So, he seys that if we expect him to forgive our mistakes, we must forgive the mistakes other people make, no matter what they do."

Bird asked, "Can people do whatever they want to do and just ask God to forgive them?" Reverend Brown shared with Bird that things are not quite that simple. He directed Bird to think about someone he really loved. Bird thought about his mama. The minister said he bet that Bird's mama had done some things that Bird did not like. He questioned Bird, "If someone was trying to hurt or kill her, would you try to stop them?"

FATHERLESS

Before Bird could respond, Reverend Brown added that he knew Bird would protect his mama not because she always did right, but because he loves her. The Reverend declared, "We are all God's children, and he loves all his people, even those who kill other people." Continuing to expound, Reverend Brown asked Bird if he had a daughter who had killed someone, "Would ya still love her?" Bird answered, "Yes." Then the preacher asked, "What if your daughter killed a pregnant woman?" Bird answered that he would be mad with her, but he would still love her. Reverend Brown concluded his lesson to Bird, "God doesn't always tell us why he does everything, but I am sure Nana and her baby are in heaven. We must pray and trust God. Boy, that's the best answer I got for you. Tonight, before you go ta sleep, ax God the same questions that you axed me, he might answer you."

"Answer me and not answer you," questioned Bird. "Yes, I am no more important ta God than you are. He always tells children thangs that he don't tell grown folks, especially children lack you," said Reverend Brown. Bird was eager to debate Reverend Brown about whether God favored anybody. He was about to counter when, he heard the bus horn blowing.

FATHERLESS

So, off Bird went--back to the school bus that would take him home.

During the following two weeks, grown folks in the community seem to be in a trance. They moved about sluggishly. The children of Grace had never seen their parents and neighbors not engage as a community and didn't even greet each other, talk about the weather or discuss how much cotton somebody picked? They didn't even talk about what the preacher said at Sunday church services. Teachers were also profoundly concerned that the family feud was on the edge of exploding beyond their imaginations after Nana was killed and Mamie was arrested. Some days, students were given two extra recesses.

The Davis County sheriff informed Mamie's daddy that the county did not have a female jail and, consequently, was going to transfer Mamie 200 miles away to Jackson, Mississippi, to be properly indicted, confined and adjudicated. Bewilderment turned to anger and more hell broke loose. Discovering that only one deputy was transporting Mamie to Jackson, several of Nana's relatives vowed to kill Mamie while the deputy had her in route. As a handcuffed and ankle-bound Mamie was led to the transport car, her dad grabbed a gun from his truck to protect his daughter from Nana's relatives. He had to be physically restrained by his two "big boys" and a couple of his neighbors.

In the meantime, the local telephone party line was buzzing hot with wildly embellished updates about Mamie's transport. Her nephews heard from one of his neighbors, who heard the information from her sister, who had been told by a close friend that Nana's family had dragged Mamie from the deputy's car and that they were about to set her on fire.

Only nine blacks in the entire town of Grace had telephones. They were all party-line telephones, which meant that everything shared over the telephone line could be heard simultaneously by others on the same multi-party telephone line just by merely picking up their handset. Anita Bankstown was talking to her sister in Benton, Mississippi. She made the mistake of repeating what she had been told about a bunch of Mamie's folk planning to shoot a bunch of Nana's folks. Twelve additional people in Benton on the same party line as Anita's sister heard bits and pieces of the conversation. They repeated various versions and shared what they had heard to other gossipmongers. Within a day, fabricated stories

FATHERLESS

of alleged clashes between the two families had spread like wildfire throughout the State of Mississippi.

By the time an unharmed Mamie was settled inside a Jackson jail cell, tempers were starting to cool. Reasoning appeared to be returning to Grace. Weirdly, however, carloads of strangers started hanging around town. Some were obviously families on vacation, others were newspaper and radio reporters, and many were curiosity seekers. Several kinfolks who lived in bigger Mississippi cities as Vicksburg "came to be with their kinfolks." Grace residents could barely move about without some visitor trying to get them to tell what they knew about "the pregnant girl killing" as labeled by news reporters. Because most of the citizens of Grace had a personal interest in the outcome of the trial, the county sheriff explicitly directed family members not to talk to anyone about the killings. He warned them that they may be called as witnesses during Mamie's trial and discussion of the situation could compromise them as witnesses.

FATHERLESS

#  Blood Letting

As Bird diligently tried to stop focusing on the death of Nana and her baby, he realized that his peace of mind was somehow tied into the constant talk by grown folks about the shenanigans going on in Grace since the deaths. One of the most outrageous stories was about a pair of first cousins. Cousins James Collins and Bill Beck were drinking beer at The Spot, a Negro juke joint in Davis County that offered illegal gambling, bootlegged liquor, music of the low-down dirty blues genre, and an occasional fist or knife fight. Visiting their cousins who were part of the late Nana's family, the two hailed from St. Louis, Missouri. Nana's aunts were James and Bill's mothers who sent their sons to Grace to help protect their kinfolks if the family feud worsened. After finishing off a couple of six-packs of beer at The Spot, James visualized a quick money-making scheme. Upon explaining the scheme to Bill, the two decided to put the plan into action the next day.

James borrowed a car from Nana's mother. He and Bill searched country fields in Davis County until they found a huge pecan tree. Not far off Highway to 447 and just a few yards from a blacktop road, the chosen tree had grown several thick, low hanging limbs. Their plan required making visitors think that they were residents of the Grace community. Consequently, they purchased overalls, work boots, work gloves, straw hats, some shotgun shells, two quart-sized cans of bright red dye, and two thick ropes. They added a gallon of The Spot's cheap moonshine to their stash.

After washing the overalls several times to give them a worn look, the cousins donned the overalls over borrowed work shirts they got from Nana's dad. Walking in a muddy ditch, their new boots were looking perfect to match up with their straw hats and work gloves. Hoisting a hoe and a sling blade, James and Bill started walking up the roadway toward town and in search of their first mark among the curiosity seekers still hanging around Grace.

A green van sporting California license plates slowed but passed by the two city slick cousins from St. Louis who were dressed to impersonate local country bumpkins. The vehicle was decorated with a variety of stickers, including colorful flowers, peace symbols, and love slogans. The van turned around and parked across from where the hustlers Bill and James stood. As the distinct smell of marijuana floated from the van and saturated the air, several young long-haired white people stumbled out of the van. "Those are hippies," Bill whispered to James. "Hey man, you dudes live around here, the driver asked Bill. He answered, "yas suh." The driver said, "No, no dudes, please don't call me, sir. We decided to use this time to groove with mother earth, find ourselves, and see the world. We heard there is a place near here where a lady's killer was shot, burned and hanged. My ole lady wants me to take a picture of the area so she can recreate the crime scene in her abstract art gallery. How much does it cost to see it and do you guys know how to get there?" asked one of the hippies.

In full character of an old Negro slave, Bill said, 'Suh, we luv ta take yo dere, but our boss mane won't lack nobody on his place. We could lose owl jobs if we take ya out dere." The hippie responded, "Tell you what dudes, hows about show us where it all went down? We'll give you $300 worth of bread and a pound of weed. It's kinda like tobacco, but it gets you high. If your boss finds out, you sell some, and you'll have enough paper to go to Canada or

FATHERLESS

someplace where you can be free and groove with some heavy people," the hippie explained.

"Yas suh," responded Bill. "Tho, ya gotta promise not ta tell nobody cause da police say dey wuz gon pistol whup de first purson dat disturbed some kinda scene, a crime scene or somethin lack dat." After Bill and James collected the $300 in cash and the pound of marijuana, they joined the hippies in the van and directed them to the pecan tree they had visited earlier. During the ride, the Bill and James nervously looked out the rear window as if they were worried.

Upon arrival at the pecan tree, Bill and James saw the scene they staged looked perfect and red paint stains looked like a blood bath had occurred there. The hippies were horrified at the what they thought was blood all over the ground and trunk of the pecan tree. James started narrating his tale, "Some folks had guns, knives and other weapons. They dragged the girl that did the killing from the Grace jail. They put the heartless killer on the back of a blue pick-up truck, and they beat her until she bled nearly to death. Then they put a rope around her neck and hung her like a side of beef. The rest of her blood drained in the grass ret thare," pointed the self-appointed fake tour guide.

FATHERLESS

Bill and James spotted another vehicle turning off Highway to 447 and heading their way. Bill said, "Dat's de mane dat werks fer de sheriff. We better git outta here!" They ran to the van and the hippies followed. "Right on," said the van driver as he floored the van's accelerator and sped off. The hippies arrived at the main highway and received directions from Bill and James on how to depart from the area without going through Grace. Bill and James shared the loot with their cousin Boo. Boo sealed the last leg of the scheme as driver of the car that scared the hippies into leaving town quickly. They ran some variation of the same scheme several more times before their deceased cousin's mother became curious and one day followed her nephews. She hid in the cotton field and listened while they cheated a Jewish family out of $220, plus a tip. By that time, James had added a stuttering to his repertoire. Nana's mom allowed her nephews to keep the unholy money they had collected, but that night, she made sure Bill and James were on a one-way, nonstop Greyhound Express Bus back to St Louis.

FATHERLESS

#  Lunch Time

Bird found himself more thankful than ever that he lived way out in "lost 40." At Bird's young age, the reference meant land located far away from civilization. However, to adult sharecroppers, the far-out rural areas meant the land was most likely that stolen from their ancestors and represented the United States' broken promise of 40 acres and a mule due to former slaves upon emancipation in 1865. At nine years old, Bird didn't care if it was lost land or plantation sharecropping land. He was just happy to be secluded from the high emotional pressures impacting the whole town and many of the families of students and employees at Grace Elementary.

With school, some days picking cotton and all the drama following the Nana killing, Bird found he still missed his daddy. Although his ache for Otis remained a terrible pain, he was learning to manage it by focusing on other thoughts. His mind no longer wandered off for hours thinking about Otis as much. Teachers finally started redirecting their full attention to educating students. They handed out homework every day.

When the lunch bell rang, students got a break from academics to eat their noon meal. The principal and his wife made baloney sandwiches for children who had a nickel and wanted to purchase the one slice of Wonder Bread with a half slice of meat and a little mayonnaise on it. Many times, the children who were fortunate buy or bring their lunch were often chased by gangs of other hungry children trying to snatch a bite of anything on the famous bread that would "help build strong bodies 12 ways." There was no cafeteria, but children who didn't buy or bring their lunch often went home or to nearby relatives for lunch. Bird did not have food at home to bring to school for lunch or money to buy food from the principal. Most school days meant no prepared lunch for Bird, that is, except the fruit and nuts he plucked from trees near Grace Elementary. Since the school had no real cafeteria, no real playground and still used outhouses for restrooms, Bird and many of his classmates thought their lunch period of no food was normal.

FATHERLESS

Occasionally, during his lunch period, Bird visited his Aunt Doonie 's in hopes of eating a quick meal and getting back to school in time to play with some of his friends before the bell rang to end the lunch period. Other times, because he didn't want to hear his aunts or others talking about Wilma Ann being a bad mother for not making sure he had lunch, Bird decided he would rather be hungry than have people saying he didn't have a good mother. While sitting in class, to cover the sounds of hunger from his rumbling stomach, Bird would rattle papers. There were quite a few days when Wilma Ann just did not cook.

Herman, one of Wilma Ann's brothers, decided his nephew needed to "toughened up" and learn how to hunt, fish and bring home the bacon just like any man of the house. Nine years old was a good age to teach Bird how to feed himself, according to his Uncle Herman. Bird was wary of any regiment led by his uncle. He remembered the way his uncle "cussed" him the last time they were together. Everyone in the Grace community knew how much Bird's Uncle Herman loved to hunt blackbirds, racoons, rabbits, and bears. Since Bird had never gone fishing, Uncle Herman made spending a day fishing at Beulah Lake their priority. He taught Bird how to fish. They talked, relaxed and enjoyed the calming beauty of the lake. When night began to fall, Bird was ready to go home. His Uncle Herman had other ideas.

"Boy, yer evah been camping in de woods," he asked. Bird shared with his uncle details of Principal Windom from Grace Elementary taking the newly formed a boy scout troupe's camping trip. Mr. Windom, Bird and the entire troupe became lost and had to spend the night in the woods. They had no food or water and although Mr. Windom brought a tent, no one could figure out how to set the tent up. The troupe spent the night lying on the cold ground. At the first sign of daylight, Mr. Windom gathered the boy scouts and took everyone back to Grace. Of course, that was the beginning and the end of the Grace Boy Scout Troupe, as well as the extent of Bird's camping experience.

Herman convinced Bird it would be enjoyable to spend the night in the woods if you know the woods and what you are doing. Uncle Herman mixed some oats, honey and smoked fat meat together. He spread the mixture around the area of their camp. He proceeded to show Bird how to build a campfire, clean, gut and filet a fish, and grill the fish over the fire. Each of them ate two whole white bass from their Lake Beulah cache of fish. Sleep overcame them and Bird enjoyed his best rest and deepest sleep he had ever experienced.

FATHERLESS

Although he did not know how long he slept, Bird woke up to the growling of a large brown grizzly bear standing on his hind legs less than 10 feet from the simmering campfire. As Bird began to stand up, the bear took a step toward him. Suddenly, a noise behind Bird sounded off like a bomb blast, and he felt intense heat and saw a flash of light pass by his right ear. That blast was followed by five more in rapid succession. Each time a frozen still Bird heard an explosion, the giant bear growled, stumble backward, and leaned forward. After the sixth blast, the bear gave one final lunge and fell forward about two feet in front of Bird.

Herman jumped, shouted and bellowed, "We got us a bear!" Then, he calmly told Bird he mixed ingredients and spread the mixture around their camp because he knew it would attract a bear. The bear would smell the bacon that he had placed near Bird while Bird was sleeping. The bear would see him and stand up to scare Bird away from the bacon. That's when his uncle planned to appear from his hidden location in the bushes to shoot the bear. According to his Uncle Herman, Bird would really be tougher if he thought he had faced down a bear. Furthermore, Uncle Herman would finally get the bear skin rug he wanted. Uncle Herman's logic, the rifle shots so close to his head and facing a growling bear about to eat him for a midnight supper, stunned Bird into amazing disbelief about the lengths his Uncle Herman would go to make a point. As shock set in deeper and deeper to his brain, Bird mumbled incoherently. Uncle Herman packed up their camp and secured the dead bear for pick up later with a borrowed truck. While the night was still pitched black in darkness, Herman took a rattled Bird home to Wilma Ann.

For a week, Bird had recurring nightmares. In each nightmare, the bear was eating Bird's leg. When Bird told his mama about his encounter with the bear, Wilma Ann cussed at her brother for risking her son's life. She insisted that Herman didn't have the sense that God gave a turtle. An outraged Herman responded cussing Wilma Ann, adding that she was so fat he wished he had taken her to the woods. "The bear coulda ate summa dat fat offa you and I coulda kept the bacon for myself." A steaming mad Wilma Ann replied, "No wonda all yo chilluns getting crazy checks." Herman countered, "At least all my chilluns got da same daddy." Their verbal sparring continued until Herman finally left Wilma Ann's house or she put him out. That fact depends on whether one believed Wilma Ann or Herman's version of events.

FATHERLESS

# 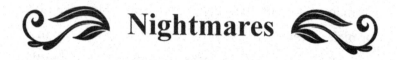 Nightmares

As Bird's nightmares increased, Wilma Ann sought medical help for her son. Her previous threats to "whip the dreams out of Bird "did not cure him. Wilma Ann appealed to her mother for help. Her family never went to the doctor and mostly used herbal concoctions to treat ailments. Bird's grandmother prescribed a remedy of three tablespoons full of her "special medicine"— the same stuff she used to treat almost everything from chicken pox to labor pains. As soon as Bird swallowed the required measurement and it hit his stomach, he felt a precious sense of calmness. He started jumping up and down with unbridled joy. When he settled down, sleep overtook his lanky, skinny body.

Upon awakening, revived with a mind of clairvoyance, Bird's first thoughts were not of a bear but of Otis. The nine-year-old quickly concluded he was lucky in some ways to not have a daddy at home. Who knows, his dad could be crazier than his Uncle

Herman. He could be a thief or robber. He could have a daddy who would force him to hunt bears and stay in the woods all night every week. Then again, Bird thought, "If my dad had been home, I would not have been in the woods with my crazy Uncle Herman."

As time passed, Bird's nightmares about the bear eating him subsided. He was finally feeling pretty good. He learned from his friends that many children on the plantation were living with their stepdaddies. Most of the friends who had them didn't like the stepdaddy arrangement. Yet, others led Bird to believe many of the stepdads were good men and he personally admired some of the ones he met. He could not imagine real dads being any better than some of his friend's stepdads.

FATHERLESS

 Fire!

One night, in the middle of his sleep, Bird awoke to Wilma Ann hitting him across his back and shouting, "Fire! Git out!" Bird collected his wits and jumped straight up out of his bed. Thick, dark smoke had consumed the kitchen and was roaring toward the middle room. Wearing only his long johns underwear with the big opening in the back-seat area, Bird reached for his pants and almost had them in his grip. His sister Mae, followed closely by Wilma Ann, ran past Bird, knocking his hand away from his pants and pushing him toward the front room. As Wilma Ann grabbed Mae by her arms and sprinted out of the house, Mae was yelling, "Mama, I wont my Bobbie doll."

"Gurl, yo bout ta git yo self-roasted lack a hog," said Wilma Ann as she flung Mae out of the front door. Bird felt a gush of hot air on his rear end as he joined the rest of his family in escaping into the night air from the heat of the fire. With the flap missing from his long johns and his rear end exposed, Bird eased his body into the field facing their house. He was hoping against hope that the cotton stalks would conceal his nakedness. Wilma Ann and two men whom Bird didn't know struggled to remove furniture, clothes and anything else they could salvage from the burning house. A few minutes later, the entire roof of the house fell to the burning floor and the raging flames swallowed the house. As the shotgun house crumpled like kindling, a voracious fire lit up the dark night. From the hand-primed water pump in the front yard to the outhouse in the back, neighbors gathered around the charred remains to help and comfort where they could or to gawk and gaze as witnesses to the traumatic event. Holding the cloth together in the back of his underwear to cover his rear end, Bird heard Wilma Ann explain to a neighbor that rats probably struck a match and set the house on fire.

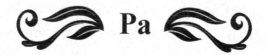

# Pa

For a third time, Bird's entire family moved in with Wilma Ann's daddy and mama. She called them Pa and Ma, as did Bird and his siblings. Ma was unusual. She was Catholic when most blacks in the Mississippi Delta were Baptist. As a creole voodoo doctor, Ma was born and raised in a small fishing hamlet near New Orleans, Louisiana. She did not like or understand most Mississippi Deltans and considered many of them to be ignorant heathens. In contrast, except for the two years he worked in New Orleans, her husband Pa lived most of his life in the Mississippi Delta.

According to Ma, her husband and daughter Wilma Ann had very similar personalities. Her other older children complained that Wilma Ann was a spoiled, gifted child and that Pa bought her everything that he could afford to get her. When he finally stopped babying Wilma Ann, she pouted for two weeks. Afterward, she ran away from home and married Willie

Jeff Davis—Retha's daddy. Her first love morphed into an abusive man whom Wilma Ann finally left before she found herself giving in to her thoughts of retaliation that ranged from poisoning his food to tying him to an coal oil soaked bed and dropping a lit match to it. She also considered cutting off his prized jewels, stabbing or shooting him right through his heart. In the end, she did shoot her first husband, but only in an area that wouldn't kill him. The shot halted his last beating attack on her.

Pa was an awesome granddaddy to Bird and his siblings. He raced with Bird, seemed to know every joke in the world and allowed Bird to be almost like his shadow everywhere he went. Pa was a well-dressed man and respected by most people in the county. Whenever he purchased a new clothing item for himself, he bought the same for Bird. While living with Pa, Bird found he didn't miss his daddy very much at all and gave no more thought to prospective stepdaddies.

As usual, Retha was still staying at her Godmother's. Bird began to notice his mother leaving home at night and returning early the next morning. Pa would not go to sleep until his daughter returned home. One morning, just before daybreak, Wilma Ann arrived home after a night of partying. Pa told her that he had put up with her "shenanigans" long enough. He explained that he let her stay out all times of the night because she was trying to find a daddy for her children. It was time for her to "do-do or git offa da pot!" Wilma Ann knew she had to obey Pa or suffer the consequences. Pa went into his bedroom and slammed the door. Wilma Ann starting crying and sat outside on the front porch in the dark until the rose pink of dawn's early light colored the morning Delta sky. The next day, Bird's mama and grandfather did not say one word to each other.

Late that night, Wilma Ann woke her children. She instructed each of them to quietly put all the personal items that they could carry in two pillowcases. Bird and his siblings followed her orders as she directed them to come with her. Bird was used to Wilma Ann's unpredictability. He suspected his mama had someone waiting outside in a car to take them to another shotgun home on another plantation. They walked out of Pa's house, quietly closed the door, and there was no car waiting. It was the darkest night that Bird had ever seen. With two pillowcases on each of their small shoulders, the three children followed Wilma Ann down the dark scary road. After about a half-mile on the route, Mae asked, "Mama, where we goin?"

"I dunno. All I know is Jezus said dat if you can't git long wit sumbady, ya neda ta shake de dust offa yore foots when ya leave dem," replied Wilma Ann. Bird was groggily half asleep as they were treading along the dark road. Wilma Ann's answer jolted him completely wide awake! Bird thought, "Lord, ya at it agin. Ya let me be happy fur a liddle time. Now ya sending me down da road wit dis crazy woman and away from da only mane dat kin handle hur."

Wilma Ann resumed, "Jezus take de wheel an lead us not into temptation but beside da still water whar da mountain holds our blessing. Ya led da chilluns of Isra ta da promised land by da nort star. Now Jezus, now Jeeezus, have yo way an senda ride ta pick us up an carrie us home. Amen." The words had barely departed Wilma Ann's lips when Pa shouted from afar, "Gal, if you don't git de chullins back ta da house, I'm gon whop ya wit dis bullwhip." Wilma Ann's eyes smiled as she turned and walked back toward Pa's house. Bird and his siblings followed, dragging their stuffed pillowcases like sacks of cotton.

Life for Bird returned to normal at Pa's house. To the chagrin of Wilma Ann's siblings, she and Pa became closer than ever. Ma said, "They wuz thick as thieves when she wuz knee hi ta a duck. Pa runt hur a long tima back. He ain't er gonna stop spoiling her now." A few weeks later, Pa suffered a heart attack and his lower body was paralyzed. Some of Pa's grown children thought his infirmed condition 'made him the perfect babysitter. They started dumping their children off at his house.

Most of Pa's grandchildren were like Bird, they just enjoyed being with Pa. The number of his grandchildren visiting sharply increased when Pa started selling candy. Some of the children decided they would steal a few pieces every day. When Pa discovered the thieves and threatened to whip them, they openly challenged him. Pa directed Bird to gather and pile up stacks of bricks near the corners of his house. Then he made sure the children knew he was placing candy near the piles of bricks. Bird was paid a nickel to roll Pa in his wheelchair around the house. Each time Pa saw one of his thieving grandchildren near the candy, he would throw bricks toward them. In just a few days of their children being unhappy and afraid to go outside, Bird's aunts and uncles decided to keep his cousins at home. Bird was thrilled that once again, he had his granddaddy all to himself.

FATHERLESS

#  The Funeral

Unfortunately, Bird's delight was short-lived. His granddaddy died the next month. While on his deathbed, Pa told Bird to always cover his head and wear two pairs of pants in the winter. Then he whispered to Bird that his daddy, Otis, was a "good man," and he would have stayed with Bird, his siblings and Wilma Ann if he could have. That was all. Pa would not discuss Otis' reasons for departure. Within a few hours, after Pa finished his soliloquy on life to Bird, his grandfather's spirit and soul departed, leaving a cold lifeless body on his bed. Like locusts buzzing about, kinfolks, friends, neighbors, associates, well-wishers, professional grievers, and curiosity seekers descended on Pa's house.

Wilma Ann's oldest sister, Zula Mae, guarded the door to her daddy's room. She wanted to prevent people from staring at Pa's deceased body. Also, she wanted to keep people from stealing his clothes until her husband and youngest brother Little Bobby could pick out what they wanted from Pa's closet. By Zula Mae's calculations, Pa had nearly 60 starched and ironed white shirts, at least 20 pairs of jeweled cuff links, more than 20 three-piece suits, and 15 pairs of Stacey Adams shoes with matching spats. Additionally, an assortment of tie clips, socks, handkerchiefs, underwear, undershirts, and bowties filled five chest drawers. Also, Pa's Dobbs hats were in protective plastic bags under his high four-post bed.

Wilma Ann was picking cotton, when Hattie Bea hollered to her the news of Pa's death. On her way home from her job as a maid, Hattie Bea was leaning out the window of the back seat of the car driven by her boss, Mrs. Amish Fowler. The car slowed just long enough for Hattie Bea to pass on the bad news. Wilma Ann threw her hands in the air and screamed, "Jezus, take me, too!" As she started running toward the highway, Wilma Ann forgot to remove from her neck the strap of the sack she was dragging through the field with some 200 pounds of cotton in it. People telling the story later said Bird's mother looked like she was the frontal wind of a tornado leaving a path of trampled cotton stalks across the cottonfield. Wilma Ann stood in the middle of the highway, determined that the next vehicle passing would get her to her daddy. The 85-year-old Pity Pat

Murphy was plodding along at 20 miles per hour in his 1946 Nash automobile and obliged to stop as Wilma Ann flagged him down.

Wilma Ann snatched the sack strap from around her neck, left her day's work on the side of the road and jumped in Pity Pat's front seat. "Drive," shouted Wilma Ann as she pointed in the direction of her Pa's house. Pity Pat obeyed. As the car pulled up at Pa's house, before Pit Pat could brake to a stop, Wilma Ann jumped out of the car and ran full speed into the house. She elbowed her way through the throng of people. Rushing into Pa's bedroom, Wilma Ann was just a couple of steps away from her daddy's bedside when two undertakers attending to him blocked her path. Lowering her head, Wilma Ann proceeded to bull-rush head-on into the smaller undertaker. Both men tumbled and fell on top of Pa as the bed broke down. Pa was lying in state on the bedroom floor!

The undertakers continued wrestling with Wilma Ann until Uncle Sonny separated them. Sonny knew all his siblings were hot-tempered and grief-stricken, therefore, it was incumbent upon him to maintain order. He instructed the undertakers to leave the room and return in an hour. Sonny ordered all non-family members to go outside for a little while, leaving the immediate family members enough room to gather inside the house.

Everyone cooperated except Minnie Littlejohn. Her son, who was almost Sonny's child, and her 12 kinfolks didn't think the "non-family member" designation applied to them. She and Sonny had lived together for a bit 10 years earlier. During the time they live together, Minnie became pregnant. Sonny was sterile by then and refused to accept Minnie's cheating on him and getting pregnant by another man. Minnie remained in full-blown denial and named her son Sonny Smith Junior. She continued to bring him to most Smith family functions and generally bugged the hell out of Sonny at every opportunity. She did so despite threats by Will Barber, her son's biological daddy, to publicly provide some details of their indiscretions to Sonny, Wilma Ann and their entire family if Minnie didn't leave Sonny alone.

Wilma Ann had finally calmed down enough to accept that Pa was gone to be with the Lord. Sonny didn't want to be rude to Minnie and her kinfolks, so he enlisted Wilma Ann to have them to leave Pa's house. Sonny ensconced himself in Pa's room. Wilma Ann walked up to Minnie and said, "Looka heah Minnie, every time sum body kicks da bucket, ya act lack a buzzard. Ya dere fore de undertakers, family or anybody else. Hell, ya might even beat death ta de purson. Now, yowl thank ya gon set a hole in my daddy's sofa and eat everthang we cook, but ya got another thought comin. Dat liddle time you spent wit Sonny is water under da bridge, it don't title ya to nuthin but sum advice, which is dis: my Pa is dead, we grieving, an if you don't leave heah ret dis minute, you might fine yoself in hell fore da devil gits da news."

"Let's go. I'll take dis up wit Sonny," responded an angry Minnie. She and her relatives gathered themselves and stormed out of Pa's house.Compared to the day of his death, Pa's funeral was somber. His sons, daughters and grandchildren were heartbroken. Wilma Ann ignored the funeral directors carefully planned order of the family line for walking up the church aisle to view Pa's body. From the opening of the church doors, she took a running start up the aisle past Ma and Uncle Sonny. She literally tried to jump into the casket with Pa. Just as Wilma Ann placed one foot inside the casket with Pa, she fainted and toppled to the church floor. Four men carried her out as ushers tried to cover her upended dress and lower body as others fanned Wilma Ann's face. Wilma Ann missed the entire funeral as she recuperated in her room at Pa's house.

Uncle Sonny put his meaty right arm around Bird's

shoulder and neck, repeatedly whispering, "Moo, Moo, Moo." Sonny's wife was squeezing Bird's right hand in a vice grip and every few minutes planted wet sloppy snuff scented kisses on Bird's right cheek. Somehow, they all made it to settle down some in the front pews designated for family members. Pa's second- oldest son Bud suddenly fell on to the floor. His show of grief was abruptly interrupted, and his balance was thrown off kilter. He wasn't looking at Pa but gazing at what the later described as the best-looking woman he had ever seen stepping up to the casket. As her curvy hips swished past Bud, he whispered to one of his friends helping him get up from the floor that the woman's "well-turned ankles" made his tears for Pa retreat into his eyeballs.

Wilma Ann's youngest sister Clemmie was drunk and tired. She snored and screamed throughout the funeral. Uncle Sonny did not get rid of Minnie. She was so overwhelmed that she wandered around the outside of the pews in a circle quoting the 23rd Psalm and eyeballing Sonny. Following Pa's burial and a short repast at the church, people gathered at Pa's house. Poor Uncle Herman, who was usually the most outgoing, boisterous, gregarious and friendliest of Wilma Ann's siblings, remained quiet and appeared lost since the day Pa died.

The family members spent the night and the

next day getting Pa's affairs in order and dividing his property. Ma was her usual quiet self, and the family decided that she would move to Arkansas with Sonny.

Except for him and his mama, during in days following Pa's funeral, Bird felt the family had forgotten about Pa. Wilma Ann was too upset to go to work and she let her children stay at home from school. Bird was in disbelief. He remained outside as much as possible as he tried to understand death and the purpose of living. Aunt Big Sis was too emotional to talk to Bird and Bird was too angry to try to communicate with God. After endless hours of contemplating and deliberating, Bird concluded caring about any living being who would eventually succumb to death was too depressing. Although he continued to do well in school as a testament to Pa's belief in his abilities, during Bird's remaining adolescent days, he became an introvert and developed a very reserved personality.

FATHERLESS

# 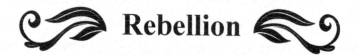 Rebellion

One hot, muggy night, Wilma Ann ordered Bird to pump four aluminum foot tubs full of water. She heated two of the containers of water on the potbelly woodburning stove and poured all the water into the big number three tub. Wilma Ann hastily took a bath, stepped out of the number three tub, and after quickly drying her body, dabbed a puff of powder on her face to help cool her sweating body. Dressing quickly, Wilma Ann donned the red suit that caused Reverend Adam Seth Teaberry to forget his sermon the first time she walked into the Morning Star Baptist Church. After dressing, Wilma Ann continued to sweat, and her face powder caked into a paste-like substance.

Mae whispered to Bird, "Mama is sweating lack a pig! Looks lack she put some cake batter on her face. Do ya thank her mine is gone?" Adjusting her red suit several times, Wilma Ann repeatedly exhaled, "Whew!" Her eyes seemed to be more crossed than usual as the left eye looked toward the front door and the other mean-looking right eye focused in the direction of Bird and Mae. "Yawl git in da bed. Ya bedder go ta sleep. It bedder be so quiet dat I bedder hear a rat peeing on cotton," she said in a scolding voice. With snide grins, Bird and Mae looked at each other and held in their laughter. They knew their mother had no idea of just how funny she looked.

Despite their mother's warning, Bird and Mae were wide awake when they heard Wilma Ann in the front room giggling. She was conversing with a male whose voice was unknown to Bird and Mae. Bird decided he needed to go to the outhouse. He walked straight through the front room and halted as he and the funny-looking stranger stared at each other. Bird recognized the stranger was one of the men he saw the morning their previous house was consumed by fire. Wilma Ann used her most affectionate tone as she smiled and said to the stranger, "Gabe, dis is my big boy Arthur." She turned to Bird and said, "Arthur dis is Mr. Gabe. He gon be stayin wit us a liddle while. He from Chicago an he needs a place ta stay."

Mr. Gabe and Bird stared at each other for a few seconds before Mr. Gabe flashed a big crooked yellow-stained toothy grin at Bird and said, "Good ta meet ya, son." Bird nodded and rushed outside as quickly as he could. He thought, "If my daddy wuz here, he would hit dat man in the mouth."

The next morning, Bird and Mae awoke to Wilma Ann's terrible crooning, but this time, instead of gospel, she was botching the words to Sam Cooke's "You Send Me." She hummed, "Darling youuu ooooh, ooooh, ooooh sen me. Ya knoe yya do., honest you do. Mmmm, mmmm, ya do, dooooo, oooo, ooooh. I fine myself wonting you, ta marry ya an take ya home.... mmmm, mmmm, ya sen me."

Bird covered his ears! The aroma of ham, the usual mixtures of varied scents, and a new odor filled the house. Stinking feet, cigarette smoke and the almost toxic air that is better known as funk floated throughout the house! Bird and Mae ate their breakfast in a hurry because they needed to get on the bus and discuss Mr. Gabe and his destiny.

During their bus ride, Bird called a meeting. "Mae, I saw da man dat mama let in our house last nite," he said. Mae asked, "What did he look lack?" Bird replied, "Lack a dog! And his feet stank. He can't stay with us!" Mae agreed. They thought about putting some rat poison in Mr. Gabe's food, but they didn't know the

FATHERLESS

exact amount to use to make him sick and not to kill him. They were also afraid that they might get caught. The two devised an alternate plan.

Wilma Ann came home and cooked a big pot of pinto beans and a big skillet of cornbread. She allowed the children to eat early. When they finished eating, Bird put a hand full of salt in the pot. They waited and watched for Mr. Gabe to return to their house. Wilma Ann invited Mr. Gabe to sit down and eat some food. She prepared a big plate of food for him. Mr. Gabe was smiling and praising Wilma Ann, but as he ate more beans, he laughed and talked less. Finally, Wilma Ann asked him if something was wrong? Mr. Gabe replied that everything was fine, but he had just remembered he needed to visit a friend. Mr. Gabe stood up and left the house. Wilma Ann looked at Bird and Mae, then she tasted her beans. "I know I didn't put dis much salt in des beans "I musta got heavy handed," she said while shaking her head and walking outside.

The next day, Bird and Mae took some of Mr. Gabe's clothes and burned them to ashes. They buried the ashes and gleefully watched as Mr. Gabe and Wilma Ann searched for his clothes. Mr. Gabe was allowed a couple days of peace because Bird and Mae wanted to be unpredictable. In the interim, one of Bird's friends told him that he overheard his daddy telling another man that Mr. Gabe had been to jail in Chicago for stealing. What great news, Bird thought. He finally had the information he needed to get rid of Mr. Gabe since Wilma Ann always preached that she detested card players, liars, and rogues. She said they are the lowest of the low. However, Bird and Mae were astounded at their mother's reaction when they informed her of Mr. Gabe's past. Wilma Ann defended the man! She explained, "Gabe wenta jail cause dey didn't lack him. Dem pecker woods up nort worse den theze down heah. Now ya need ta sta outta grown folk bizness fore, I stomp a mudhole in yo booties."

Stunned, Bird and Mae found themselves back to the drawing board with less respect for and fear of their mama. Wilma Ann had really made them mad. They decided under no circumstance would they tolerate any man except relatives living in their house. They considered various poisons, but they still had no idea of how much would make Mr. Gabe as sick as a dog without killing him. Fortune presented the children with a new opportunity. Mr. Gabe left a pair of his fancy shoes near the front door. Bird and Mae placed the shoes very close to the wood-burning heater. The shoes' leather curled from the heat and the pair was ruined. Mr. Gabe was

FATHERLESS

very angry with Wilma Ann and demanded to know if she was trying to run him off. The two exchanged some harsh words and Wilma Ann suddenly turned toward Bird and Mae.

Wilma Ann grabbed Bird by his collar. With a balled fist, she shouted, "Boy, you an yo fat assed suster thank yawl smart! I bet a dollar gainst a dime dat yawl behind everthang dat happen to Gabe. One a yawl gon tell me de trufh or I'm gon whup ya'all so bad till yawl gon lack it so good till yawl gon beg me ta kill ya." As their mother drew back her fist as if she were going to hit them, Bird and Mae stood tall and did not flinch or shy away from her threat. The siblings decided that they would not snitch on each other and nor would they confess to anything. Most importantly, Bird and Mae had made up their minds to not let Mr. Gabe live in the house with them.

Maybe Wilma Ann admired their resolve, possibly Mr. Gabe did not need the added tension, or perhaps divine intervention occurred. Wilma Ann straightened out her fisted fingers, released Bird's collar, turned and walked toward Mr. Gabe. "Gabe," she said, "I'll see ya later." Mr. Gabe gathered what was left of his belongings and exited their front door. Bird and Mae never saw him again.

FATHERLESS

#  Fat Sam

Wilma Ann waited a few months before she tried dating again. The next man she brought home was Fat Sam. Wilma Ann must have groomed him for the dissension he was about to face. He came in the door bearing gifts--giving Mae a Barbie doll and dollhouse and blessing Bird with a harmonica, guitar and a set of drums! Otha was presented with a "have gun will travel" toy gun and holster. Wilma Ann's children were amazed. It was almost like Christmas! Fat Sam had a nice car, too. He told Bird he was going to teach him how to drive. Fat Sam spent a couple nights skinning and grinning at their house. Although Bird and Mae figured him out quickly, they decided to tolerate the man if the goodies kept coming.

Fat Sam left to go Memphis and promised to bring Bird a bicycle back with him. Bird really wanted that bicycle. So, he spent the weekend trying to convince Mae that they needed to be a little kinder to Fat Sam if he brought back a new bike for Bird. Fat Sam returned from Memphis with a warm, charming smile, a new dress for Wilma Ann, a toy watch for Mae, and a yo-yo for Otha. Wilma Ann listened with great interest as Fat Sam gave a long, detailed speech to Bird explaining that he paid for the bike, but the store was closed when he went back to pick it up. There was no reason to worry, he planned to bring the bike back on his next Memphis trip.

Bird wanted the bike so badly until he allowed himself to believe Fat Sam. His sister Mae quickly brought him back to reality. Mae said, "Mr. Fat Sam ain't brought ya no bike. He ain't left no money at no stoe. He jests wont ta fool ya. Bird was so exasperated that he had allowed himself to be deceived. The feeling of ambivalence about Fat Sam morphed into something resembling a passionate hate. Fat Sam needed a lesson, Bird decided.

Bird noticed an odor in Fat Sam's car that drove mosquitoes into a frenzy. The car did not have an air conditioner which resulted in Fat Sam profusely sweating. His perspiration penetrated the leather seats and made the car a mosquito magnet. The stinging pests made high pitched humming sounds that grew louder around the car. While his family and Fat Sam were asleep, Bird sneaked outside and slightly rolled down all the windows on Fat Sam's shiny tan Ford Thunderbird. Swarms of mosquitoes took over the car's interior as Bird eased back into the house and quietly returned to bed.

Bird didn't tell Mae about his ploy because he thought Wilma Ann definitely would whip somebody after she learned of the damage. He wanted to spare his sister this one inevitable whipping. Although Saturday morning was a time when Bird enjoyed typically enjoyed languishing in bed and sleeping late, he rose early to witness Fat Sam's reaction to a car full of mosquitoes. Fat Sam was an early riser, too. He had just finished a big breakfast and patted his big belly as he headed to his car. As Fat Sam was driving away, Bird saw the car come to a sudden stop. Fat Sam jumped out of his vehicle while swinging and hitting himself as he tried to ward off the cloud of blood sucking mosquitoes surrounding and biting him.

Fat Sam left his car running as he hustled back to Wilma Ann's house. After listening to Fat Sam's description of what happened, Wilma Ann immediately focused her evil eye on Bird. Scratching her head, she grabbed her spray gun and went outside to the running car where she sprayed the inside with heavy blasts of the Black Flag bug killer. Fat Sam made the ironic decision that it would be better for him to live in town instead of out in the boonies with Wilma Ann, her kids and all those blood sucking mosquitoes.

She had no proof, but Wilma Ann insisted that Bird and Mae had something to do with Fat Sam moving out of their house.

# 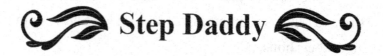 Step Daddy

Wilma Ann's next attempt at romance was with a man named Jack Bodie. He came to their house one day and Wilma Ann introduced him to Bird and Mae. She said, "Mr. Bodie, des two liddle ones is my chullins Arthur and Mae. Ya keep your eye on dem. Dey low down. Dey'll thow bricks at cha an hide dey hanes, but if'n dey give ya any trouble, you kin git Jimmy the undertaker, cause dey gon be dead as a doe knobs." Mr. Bodie didn't say anything as he nodded his head and politely smiled at Bird and Mae.

Mae told Bird that Mr. Bodie had kindness in his eyes. Bird hadn't noticed the kindness, but he realized Mr. Bodie seemed different from Wilma Ann's other recent love interests. Mr. Bodie was well-dressed, very polite and articulate. He lived in a nearby town, but he did not own a car. Sometimes, on the weekends, Mr. Bodie stayed late at Wilma Ann's house, but he never spent the night. Mae really liked him, but Bird remained aloof and distant.

Anytime Bird found himself becoming more accepting of Mr. Bodie, he reminded himself about lying Fat Sam. After Mr. Bodie and Wilma Ann had dated for about a month, Mr. Bodie found himself in a predicament and had little choice but to spend the night at their house. The man he rode to town with was too drunk to pick Mr. Bodie up that night and did not come to get him until the next morning. Despite Mr. Bodie sleeping in his clothes, Bird considered the situation as a ploy by his mama. Wilma Ann had previously convinced Mr. Bodie to leave some clothes at her house in case he needed them on a future visit. On the day following Mr. Bodie's ride finally picking him up, Bird decided he had work to do. Attempting to replicate the way a rat would eat a shirt, Bird cut tiny holes in one of Mr. Bodie's dress shirts. The Friday when Mr. Bodie returned, he and Wilma Ann were getting ready to go to town when they discovered the holes in the shirt. Wilma Ann grabbed Mae and threatened to make her sleep outside in the cotton field all night if she did not tell her what happened to the shirt. Mae was afraid of the dark. If she had known, she surely would have confessed. Bird was glad he had not discussed his scheme with anyone.

FATHERLESS

Mr. Bodie quickly intervened during their mama's tirade. He said, "Ms. Wilma Ann, I just remembered that this is a shirt I was going to throw away because the rats got in my house and they ruined it." He apologized to Mae and Bird for being so much trouble and for staying the night at their home without talking to them. Wilma Ann responded, "Now, look heah, Mr. Bodie, ya don't need ta explain nuthin ta dem. Dis is my house. I pay all da bills heah! If ya notice, ya never see a tail wagging a dog, da dog is always wagging da tail. In dis house, I'm da dog, they da tails!"

After their mother and Mr. Bodie left, Mae said, "See, I tole ya he wuz a nice man, too nice for mama." Later, Mr. Bodie asked Bird to take a short walk with him. After they had traveled a short distance, Mr. Bodie stopped and looked directly into Bird's eyes. "Son, I know your daddy, and I like him, and I know that I'm not your daddy and I'm not trying to be him. I'm not blessed enough ta have any children of my own, but if I had children, I would want them ta be jest like you and your sister. I met yo mama before she got with your daddy. We use ta to be close. I thought one time that she was going ta be my wife. I've loved ya mama since the first time I met her. I'm gon do everything in my power ta make her happy until your daddy comes back.

FATHERLESS

"Wilma Ann don't feel the same way about me, and I know yawl have had some hard times without your daddy," he continued. I know how ya feel. My daddy left me when I was nine years ole and I never saw or heard from him again. Then, my mama died when I was 10. I didn't have any sisters or brothers. I was raised from house ta house with anybody that would put a roof over my head and feed me. I stayed mad about something all the time and quickly wore out my welcome everywhere I went. When I was 17, I ran off and joined the Marine Corps. That's where I learned ta be a man. Now I know that ya mad about yo life an what Otis did ta ya by leaving. All I can tell ya is that he had ta leave the way that he did. If he had another way, he would've taken it. The rest, he'll have ta tell you an I believe that he will one day. I'm gon try ta help ya, but I would count it as a great favor ta me if ya would not cut up my clothes," Mr. Bodie said. He extended his right hand for Bird to shake. This time, Bird saw the kindness in his eyes. Bird wanted to hug the kind man and never turn him loose. Instead, his pride prevailed, and Bird humbly shook Mr. Bodie's colossal hand and nodded.

Bird and Mr. Bodie started spending more time together. On his weekend visits to Wilma Ann, Mr. Bodie always remembered to bring plenty of candy to her children. However, Wilma Ann seemed to have an issue with Mr. Bodie. One day she asked him if he came to see her or her children?  Maybe Wilma Ann was not getting enough attention from Mr. Bodie, or perhaps there was some other concern. Two or three times a week, Wilma Ann began dressing in her church clothes and leaving home at night. Usually, her children were asleep by the time she returned home.  One night, Bird was awake when another man they did not know brought their mom home in a car. Mae and Bird became upset. Their mama had finally found a kind man in Mr. Bodie and she was about to mess it up!

Mr. Bodie apparently suspected Wilma Ann was cheating on him because he showed up at their house in the middle of the week. He asked the man who drove him there to wait with him until Wilma Ann came home. After about four hours passed, Mr. Bodie addressed Bird, explaining he was starting to worry about their mama and asked if he knew where she might be.

Bird quietly consulted with Mae and they concluded Mr. Bodie had enough tension from Wilma Ann. Not only did they tell Mr. Bodie what he asked, but they went on to tell him about Wilma Ann's frequent trips away from home. In hopes of keeping the kind Mr. Bodie around to straighten their mama out, Bird and

Mae embellished their stories with a flagrant disregard for truth. They said a different man brought their mama home every night.

Mr. Bodie asked his driver to take him to town. Bird hoped Mr. Bodie would scare the devil out of his mama and humble her a little. Most likely, Wilma Ann was at a café dancing and laughing without a care in the world. Bird and Mae happily imagined all the ways that Wilma Ann was going to react when Mr. Bodie surprised her. Wilma Ann arrived home about 3:30 a.m. the next day. She hurried through the front door with Mr. Bodie close on her heels. Mr. Bodie shouted, "Ya can run, but ya can't hide."

Bird and Mae walked in the kitchen just as Mr. Bodie whispered into Wilma Ann's left ear. Whatever he said seemed to uncross Wilma Ann's eyes. She looked straight at Mr. Bodie and said, "Jack, dat main wuz my cousin an we fool folks lack we lack each other. I'm gon stop playin wit him lack dat fore ya git yo self in trouble." Mr. Bodie responded, "Little girl, ya did the same thing ta me years ago when I caught ya that time. The man was supposed ta be yo cousin. Ya a little too close ta ya kinfolks for me. Then, ya out all times of night, leaving ya small children. The house could've caught on fire or something. So, I'm going ta stay away from here."

FATHERLESS

Wilma Ann seemed a little sad, but she quickly composed herself. She screamed at Mr. Bodie,"Ya talk lack it wuz quitin time when da good Lord made ya an he didn't make no more men after dat! You kin stay at yo house, cause I wuz lookin fer a main when you met me."

Mr. Bodie did not respond. He apologized to Bird and Mae for waking them up. He said he lived alone and if they ever need him to let their uncle know. Since their uncle came by his grocery store almost every day, he would let Mr. Bodie know if the children needed him. Mr. Bodie hugged Bird, Mae and Otha, said goodbye and left. Mae started crying. She said, "Arthur, now Mr. Bodie ain't gon be branging us no mo candy from his stoe." The two regretted telling Mr. Bodie about Wilma Ann since it was at the root of them a losing out on a lot of cookies, candy and other goodies. For days after she and Mr. Bodie called it quits, Wilma Ann was quiet or humming her gospel songs. "Precious Lawd, take my hane, lead me on, oooooh, let me stan. I's tied, I's weak...," she whimpered. Definitely, she was no Mahalia Jackson, but Wilma Ann was somber and deep in her feelings as she started wailing through a new song. "Sooonnnn, I'll be done with tha troubles n tha werld! Soonnnn...."

Bird and Mae almost felt a little sorrow for their mama as they heard her singing, but they were joyous about

FATHERLESS

finally getting some peace in their home. They laughed as quietly as they could and suggested to each other that they should be the ones singing. Mahalia Jackson's "How I Got Over," would be their song of choice!

#  Log Head Red

The children's peace was short-lived. As they got off the school bus one Monday afternoon, an odd-looking short man was sitting on the steps of their front porch. "Hey chullins, is dis whar Wilma Ann stay?" Bird and Mae suspiciously hesitated and answered simultaneously, "Yessir."

"My name is Fredricka Ross, but everybody calls me Log Head Red, causa my skin color an causa I been cutting an hauling logs since I was knee-high to a June bug. Tell ya, mama dat um going ta town ta git a beer an I be back directly," he said as he headed to his car. Then he drove away. When Wilma Ann made it home, Bird gave her Mr. Red's message and went to bed. The next morning Bird was startled awake by the sound of someone banging on their front door. As Bird stumbled to the door, Wilma Ann and Mr. Red were already standing in the doorway. Wilma Ann was talking to a white lady who was standing on the other side of the door's threshold. "Good morning Mrs. Sanders. Kinda early ain't it," said Wilma Ann.

"Well, yawl go to the fields so soon until this time of day is the best time ta catch yawl at home," replied the white lady. "It's time for ya ta get re-certified for your commodities and welfare check. But ya seem to have a man in ya house. I need to find out about him or I'm gon have to cut yawl off."

Wilma Ann took a solid stance in the middle of the doorway, placed her hands on her hips and with full affirmation of her adultness, said "Da $27 a month an da commodity food is fer the chullins, but the maine is for me! Yawls give us some meat dat des dogs won't eat, cheese dat block ya bowels fer a mont, and some powder milk dat have ya runnin over folks ta git ta da outhouse! Den, yawl don't wont no sangle woman ta have nothin ta do wit a main? Now, each woman at yo welfare office goes home ta her maine everie nite. So, ya keep da liddle check and the commodities and stay the hell away from my house, cause I kin hustle up on mo den dat by my darn self!" Wilma Ann took one step back and slammed the door in Mrs. Sanders face!

Wilma Ann was so ticked off at the welfare woman that she decided not to work in the cotton field

FATHERLESS

that day. She and Mr. Red stayed at home all day. Bird and Mae had a quick meeting while they were at school. They decided Mr. Red would have to be sent away from their home, too.

While Wilma Ann and Mr. Red were out on the town that night, Bird and Mae gathered and bundled Mr. Red's clothes into a bedsheet. They dropped the bundle into the small creek near their house. Reveling in a belief that Wilma Ann would never discover their role in Mr. Red's disappearing clothes, Bird and Mae practiced potential explanations to have ready in case their mother pressured them.

The following morning, as Mr. Red was preparing to dress for work, he discovered all his work clothes were missing. Out of patience with her children trying to run off any man she liked, Wilma Ann swung her fist to hit Bird in his face. Bird ducked just in time. Mr. Red grabbed Wilma Ann before she could throw another punch at her son's head. He went on to convince Wilma Ann that he would persuade the children to get along with him.

Mae and Bird decided to match wits with Mr. Red and let him think that he could handle them. Mr. Red had his own plan. He brought Wilma Ann's entire family new clothes, and he treated Bird and Mae to all the hamburgers

FATHERLESS

that they could eat. Every day that he came to their house, he brought something for each child. Sometimes, it was tasty food and other times, it was toys. He seemed to want to spoil Wilma Ann, Bird, Mae and little Otha. Bird and Mae became the envy of other Easter Road children.

Mr. Red drove a candy apple red 1955 Chevrolet Bel Air convertible. It had a fascinating design and sported a Chevy V-shaped benchmark engine with eight cylinders! Mr. Red loved to drive and to drive fast. Cars were his passion. Not only was Mr. Red self-taught on auto mechanics, but he was also known as one of the best persons in the auto body and paint business. He always kept pretty cars. The local white police systematically harassed Mr. Red because of his fancy looking automobiles. Their harassment included publicly bullying Mr. Red who suffered a speech impediment and stuttering during tense situations.

Mr. Red's reputation preceded him. Before courting Wilma Ann, he still helped his ex-wife out a couple of Saturday mornings each month by taking her to and from the grocery store. Among the community's many legends about Mr. Red was his relationship with the local law enforcement. The police often concocted traffic stops designed to explicitly harass Mr. Red. On one Saturday morning, with his convertible top down,

Mr. Red pulled up to the concocted traffic stop with his ex-wife sitting in the passenger seat. Without saying a word, the officer marched up to the sleek convertible and pimp-slapped Mr. Red right across his cheek. Before the policeman could draw his hand back from Mr. Red's face, Mr. Red pulled a knife from his pocket and sliced the policeman's wrist. As the second officer started to draw his revolver, Mr. Red grabbed a German Lugar gun from under his car seat and threated to shoot both officers if they did not leave him alone. Mr. Red grabbed the officers' guns and sped away.

In addition to his many other skills, Mr. Red was quite comfortable in wooded areas. He earned part of his living by sawing logs at a logging camp. When he received news that the police were planning to kill him, Mr. Red left his logging job and went to work on a tugboat that hauled logs on a barge up and down the Mississippi River. He slept on the boat and avoided socializing in towns where the boat docked. A year later, Mr. Red decided to quietly slip into town unnoticed. His first stop was at his first wife's home.

Someone tipped the police off about Mr. Red's plans. Prison guards, sheriff's deputies, constables, town marshals, jailers, dispatchers and others affiliated with law enforcement were invited by the local police to join them in capturing or killing Mr. Red. Minutes after Mr. Red had settled down to have a meal, the mob of gunmen surrounded the house and ordered Mr. Red to surrender. Upon negotiating to allow his former wife to leave the premises and after she was safely away from harm, Mr. Red rushed out the front door of the house firing a shotgun in one hand and his German Lugar in the other. A flying buck shot pellet touched the ear of Roy Percy Gould, the local game warden. He urinated on himself and broke his nose as he fell face first to the ground. While Roy laid on the ground moaning, Wilson Petrel and Dan Stobart, were indecisive. They really wanted to exact revenge for the humiliation Mr. Red had caused them by taking their guns. However, they decided retreating was the better part of valor for them. As fast as they could move, followed closely by an entire posse of armed men, Officers Petrel and Stobart stood down as Mr. Red escaped. When the chaos eased, a fellow game warden found Roy kneeling on a log near the shootout. Roy had just turned his soul over to Jesus Christ.

#  Wolf Tickets

Although Mr. Red's car was almost six years old, he washed it practically every day. Prospective buyers were always making offers to him for the car. Bird was happy Mr. Red rejected all the offers because Bird really enjoyed the sleek and powerful vehicle. Most Sundays, after Wilma Ann came home from church, Mr. Red took her and her children on afternoon drives. Wilma Ann and Mr. Red were really beginning to like each other. Mr. Red started introducing Wilma Ann as his wife and Bird as his "son-in-law," although he meant "stepson." He taught Bird how to drive and occasionally gave Bird the keys to his car with five dollars of spending money. Wilma Ann intervened each time "to keep Bird from ending up in Timbuktu," she explained.

Approaching 11 years of age, Bird began to consider that he might be betraying his daddy by becoming close to Mr. Red. For some undefined reason—perhaps love or maybe enchantment, Bird's mind would always return to the thought that Otis was coming back for him and the rest of his family. Of course, that meant Mr. Red needed to go. His confidante sister Mae was not around as much because she was now spending more time with her godmother than with Bird and Otha. As much as he liked Mr. Red, Bird wanted his real daddy Otis in his life more than he wanted a stepdaddy relationship with Mr. Red.

Bird commenced to finding out as much as he could about Mr. Red in order to run the man off without physically hurting Mr. Red. Bird discovered not only had Mr. Red been in the legendary police shootout that people generally talked about in his community, but he had been in a second shootout with another police department where was convicted of six counts of assault with a deadly weapon on a police officer. For those offenses, Mr. Red spent 10 years in prison. As Bird gathered his arsenal of information, he learned more positive news than he wanted to hear. Mr. Red fought in the Korean War and was decorated for bravery. Mr. Red was a tireless worker who consistently labored at several jobs. Ironically, the additional information Bird learned about Mr. Red's past, the more Bird appreciated him.

Mr. Red loved to be around music and dancing. He convinced Wilma Ann to move to the Town of Asher and out of the shotgun house for sharecroppers. They moved into another shotgun house, but this time, located directly in front of Ettie Mack Mae's Cafe, the busiest juke joint in Asher. During the weekends, Ettie Mack sold beer and grocery items and made small loans. From 3:00 o'clock Friday evenings to 3:00 o'clock Monday mornings, Ettie Mack was in the juke joint business. Most of the customers were poor black sharecroppers looking for cheap entertainment. Ettie Mack did not disappoint them. Aside from singing, dancing, drinking and good food, there were many quarrels and occasionally a dispute that ended in a homicide.

Mr. Red was very happy because of the convenience in dropping by Ettie Mack's place every day after work to have a beer before crossing the street to go home. Wilma Ann was pleased because she liked blues music and the excitement of the weekend crowds that gathered at Ettie Mack's. Bird was miserable because he forced to endure loud, profane language and blues music almost all night on Fridays and Saturdays.

Mr. Red was usually right in the middle of the club's activities as speakers amplified the blues from the colorful jukebox. Patrons also gambled as they drank alcohol, cussed, told jokes, and had a good time away from the stress of the cotton fields and the pressures of racism. Often, Mr. Red would come home drunk, give Bird a handful of loose change and habitually try to get the 11-year-old to drive him to another juke joint before sleep overtook him.

On one such night, Bird overheard Mr. Red and another man arguing. The men threatened to shoot each other. Knowing Mr. Red's history of violence, Bird slipped out the back door of their house to try to get Mr. Red to come home. Bird was much relieved when he discovered the two men were talking smack, and in fact, they were longtime friends. They had just met up again and were "selling wolf tickets" to each other as a long-practiced cultural ritual of men who were very good friends getting reacquainted.

# 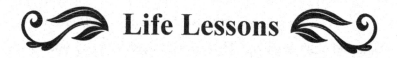 Life Lessons

Bird discovered he could slip out at night without anyone knowing.  He would attempt to sleep during the early nighttime hours when there were just a few patrons at Ettie Mack's.  Around midnight, Bird would slip outside of their home and concealed himself in the middle of the tall, dense grass between his house and the juke joint. Bird watched and listened to grown folks that he had once respected and admired.  They were sinning every which way--getting drunk, spewing profanities and shooting dice on the ground just outside the of the juke joint. Ettie Mack's had no air-conditioning; therefore, patrons continuously came outside to cool themselves and pursue more private interactions.

From Bird's vantage point, he was not only entertained, but also gained an interesting street-smart education.  He  saw Deacon Banks trying to give Mary Belle five dollars for sex, heard mother Hattie tell mother

Georgia that she had a baby by Reverend Haley, and he heard the Moakley boys talk about how they put holes in some of their neighbors' outhouses to peek at females using the toilet. Bird was shocked at some of the things he heard, especially from people he once respected and admired. In the end, Bird decided to stop spying. It occurred to him he would be mad if someone secretly overheard him and Mae discussed deeds that they had done to run off their mama's various male friends.

Bird's new hobby focused on gathering whisky bottles, beer cans, cigarette butts, dice and playing cards that were discarded near the juke joint. Bird sipped the small amounts of beer and whiskey left in the discarded bottles and cans and he smoked the cigarette butts. Bird learned to play cards, shoot dice and cuss. After Bird bragged about his late-night exploits to his friends, Mr. Red discovered what his "stepson" was doing. He strongly advised Bird to stop before Wilma Ann heard about his disgusting activities. Mr. Red's warning came too late.

Wilma Ann showed up at Bird's school and informed his teacher that she needed to take Bird outside to talk to him. The moment they stepped outside of the school doors, Wilma Ann pulled out the extension cord she had concealed in her purse. She whacked Bird with the cord, leaving an inch-wide welt across his right shoulder. Seconds later, Bird was stunned by a delayed sharp pain from the first lick of the extension cord as he raised his hand to shield an oncoming second lick. Wilma Ann struck Bird with the extension cord on his left leg. Her strategic whacks threw Bird off balance. By the time Mr. Windom, the school principal, stopped Wilma Ann, Bird had welts all over his body. While she was resting, Bird's mama declared to Mr. Windom that she would not have a gambler, liar, rogue, or a person who ravishes women as a son. She went on to share with Mr. Windom some of what she had heard about Bird's juke joint activities. The principal and Bird's teacher Ms. Baker pleaded with Wilma Ann to get her to stop whipping Bird. The explained that her son was one of the most obedient, courteous and intelligent children in the entire school. Ms. Baker further expressed her hope to one day be lucky enough to have a child as bright and wonderful as Bird.

Upon hearing the admiration widely respected educators had for her son, Wilma Ann's entire demeanor changed. Her mouth unfurled. The anger left her eyes and she became almost giddy. It was the first time Bird had seen his mother show some pride in him. Wilma Ann made sure that the entire black population and a few white people in their town knew that the teacher had bestowed greatness upon her son. According to Wilma Ann's embellished version, the teachers claimed her son was the best student they had ever seen. Furthermore, they thanked her for all the hard work she had singlehandedly put into Bird to make him a boy of whom she could be proud.

For the first time in the school's history, Grace Elementary established a 4-H Club and Mr. Windom appointed Bird as the club's first president. Wilma Ann behaved as if Bird had been elected president of the United States of America. She went to yard sales in the white community and brought nice second-hand clothes for Bird so he would look like the leader he was meant to be. From Wilma Ann's new attitude, Bird learned that his value to his mother depended greatly on the accolades about him that she received from others.

Bird found a big box of Hip magazines in a large uninhabitable room in the back of their house. Hip Magazine marketed to black teenagers' girls. It discussed topics such as ways to repel sexual advances, when should a girl go all the way, how to find out if a girl loved her boyfriend, and similar subjects. Bird's new hobby was to become an expert on girls. When he tried out the roses are red, violets are blue sure-fire technique on Jean

Farris, she laughed him out of her yard. Obviously, the folks in Hip Magazine didn't know anything about the girls where he lived, concluded Bird.

Initially, Bird was disturbed to see many deacons of the church cussing and talking about what they had done or were going to do with various women. As time passed, Bird did not see a difference between the partying people and the church people until Sunday mornings. While wine heads were lying on somebody's porch drunk, the holy rollers of churches were hung over while sitting in the church pews. However, Reverend Brown continued to be a ray of hope. He sometimes confessed to his church members that he was not perfect. He said sometimes, he liked to drink a little wine and listen to some blues. He advised his congregation to stop judging and start encouraging each other because God is the only one righteous enough to be fair.

FATHERLESS

#  Daddy's Home

Later in the week, Bird was behind their home practicing his profanity skills when he heard Mae calling for him. As he headed toward her and rounded the house, she was on the front porch pointing to an unfamiliar car parked in front of their home. Bird, with his protective attitude about his family, strolled toward the car as its passenger windows were rolled down. A large man sat in the driver's seat, a woman and a small girl were in the front passenger seat and two small boys peeked out of the windows from their seats in the back of the car. The man stepped out of the car and looked at Bird. He asked, "Is this Annie's house?" Bird shook his head and answered "no sir" as he walked back toward the front porch of their home.

The man got back in his car, but he did not drive away. The woman shouted, "Are you Arthur and is this

FATHERLESS

Wilma Ann's house?" Bird pretended to not hear the woman as he went inside the house to get his mother. He told Wilma Ann some strangers were outside asking questions about him and somebody named Annie. Wilma Ann peeked out the screen door and immediately ran toward the back room. She grabbed a pail and told Bird to run outside and bring back some water. As Bird returned to the house with a pail of water for his mother, he saw Mae talking to the man in the car. After pouring the water he had drawn from the outdoor pump into the tub for Wilma Ann to take a quick bath, Bird went back outside. The man and his passengers were all out of the car and heading toward Bird. As the man was speaking to Bird again, Wilma Ann flung open the screen door and stepped onto the porch. Dressed in her church clothes and with her wig sitting backward on her head, she ran up to the man, grabbed his hand and said, "Dit, hi ya done?"

The man replied, "Fine Annie" and peeled his hand out of Wilma Ann's grasp. Her eyes bucked and a big grin spread across Wilma Ann's face. Bird was surprised. Obviously, the man was his daddy! Wilma Ann had criticized Otis for years and Bird was very disappointed in her sudden lap dog behavior. She didn't cuss, fuss or frown.

FATHERLESS

Otis' female companion introduced herself as his wife and made sure everyone knew the children with her belonged to Otis. She emphasized that the little girl "was his heart." Wilma Ann's smile quickly vanished, and she said, "Mae, Arthur, dis is ya daddy." She walked back into the house and slammed the front door.

Otis made small talk with Bird, Mae and Otha for about 30 minutes before he gave them his address in Jackson, Tennessee. As he drove away with his new family. Wilma Ann's children were not bother at all to see their daddy leave. In only a few minutes, they realized Otis might be their daddy,.but he was a stranger to them. Mae and Otha vowed to never see Otis again. They kept their promise.

FATHERLESS

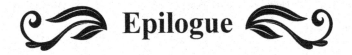

# Epilogue

When Bird's first child was born, he visited Otis to let him know he was a grandfather. Bird told his father he had forgiven him for abandoning him and his siblings. Otis shared with Bird why he left. He said that he was always planning to leave Mississippi and taking his family with him. His plans were ruined when Mr. Hobbs called him "boy." Otis said he asked Mr. Hobbs to stop calling him boy and informed the plantation owner of Otis being his name, not boy.

Asking Otis if he remembered Emmett Till, Mr. Hobbs accused Bird's daddy of being a smart mouth nigger. As the plantation left to get the county sheriff, Otis thought about some of the men he worked with who had been falsely convicted, sent to prison and later leased or paroled out of prison to be managed by various farmers in the Delta as unpaid workers. Otis continued recapping the day he left his family in

Mississippi. He reminded his son that he woke him, Mae and Otha up and told them that he loved them and assured them he was coming back one day to get them. Otis realized Mr. Hobbs had almost every police officer in the Delta looking for him as he traveled back roads and levees all the way to Memphis.

Otis said he was broke and tired, but he hopped rides on freight trains and traveled across the United States to work odd jobs until he felt Hobbs was no longer looking for him. Two years later, he slipped back in Mississippi to get his family, but found Wilma Ann did not want to leave her ailing daddy. Still planning to try again the next year when the time was right, but complications arose due to falling in love with another woman and Wilma Ann being committed to someone else, too. Although almost five long years had passed since the day Bird and his siblings saw Otis, the day did come when Otis fulfilled his promise to come back for his children. Bird's parents never got back together as a family.

Well into her 70s, Wilma Ann took her last breath while surrounded by a room full of family and friends. Over the years, Otis divorced and remarried several times. He died alone at the age of 52 in a rooming house in Tomb, Tennessee.

## FATHERLESS

Retha had several children before she married and divorced her last child's father. She never trusted men and was always fearful of not having any money. She worked for the same company for 45 years without missing a day or even being late. A few years after retiring, she lost the fight for her life to congestive heart failure.

Otha never really knew Otis. At the age of 10, he was run over by a tractor and suffered severe brain damage. By the time Otha was 18, he was in the pipeline of spending much of the rest of his life in prison.

Mae decided she was never going to marry. After all, a man could abandon his family just like her daddy Otis abandoned her, her siblings and her mother.

Bird grew up and learned to cherish the times that he and his daddy spent together as adults. He married, worked and helped to raise his family. He made sure that his children knew that he loved them and that they could always depend on him to be there for them. He came to understand his mother Wilma Ann much better. Consequently, he grew to admire her courage, faith, and determination. While his childhood was focused on a storybook enchantment of having his father in his life, he came to realize the real powerful force in his life.

As an adult, Bird continues to smile at the thought of the enchanting, colorful, strong-willed and sometimes wacky woman who worked tirelessly to provide for him and his siblings. His mother supplied plenty of entertainment along the way. Wilma Ann was unique as the single hard-working parent who worked 12-hour days in the cottonfields to do her best in providing and caring for her family in the Jim Crow South.

FATHERLESS

# Wilma Ann's Glossary & Translations

A hard head makes a soft butt – *stubbornness in a youth who is destined for many whippings to sensitize his or her buttocks*

A shame fore God - *the worst kind of offense*

Alla - *all of something*

Axed – *asked*

Belly washer - *a 16-ounce soft drink*

Bird brain - *a stupid person*

Bird legs - *skinny legs*

Block ya bowels - *constipation*

Booties - *buttocks*

Chilluns - *children*

Colored – *a term referring to Americans of African descent*

Dat - *that*

Dey - *they*

Dis - *this*

Do-do or git off de pot - *make a serious decision*

Fast tail/fastness – *overly friendly girl*

Goin outta style - *will no longer exist*

Gurl - *girl*

Heah - *hear*

Jesus take de wheel - *a request for immediate divine help*

Lack – *as if; like*

Late night nurse – *an illicit girlfriend*

Liddle - *little*

Lordy - *Lord*

Love ya in Christ - *love you as a fellow Christian*

Nack - *neck*

No count - *a bad person or thing*

Offa - *off of*

Peckerwood - *a derogatory term referring to a Caucasian*

Playing the dozens - *telling jokes about someone's mother*

Plez - *please*

Prayer warrior - *a person whose prayers got a quick response from God*

Roguish - *a thief*

Running all over folks ta get to git ta de out house - *diarrhea*

Sense that god gave a coon - *a person of below average intelligence*

Sey - *say*

Spray gun - *a hand size tin canister with an extended handle used to emit liquid poison in the form of a spray*

Stoe - *store*

Straighten up an fly right - *make a positive change*

Werk - *work*

Wit - *with*

Wolf tickets - *verbal threats without action*

Wuz - *was*

Yawl - *you all*